Praise for *Tarot by Tempest*

"Tempest's perspective is uniquely refreshing, offering readers an intuitive and embodied way to engage with the cards.... She is one of the most insightful and influential magickal voices of our time, and this book is a vibrant expression of her vision and understanding of the tarot."
—MAT AURYN, author of *The Psychic Art of Tarot* and *Psychic Witch*

"Zakroff cuts through Tarot's clutter with a system that's lean, striking, and alive with pattern. It turns every deck into a tool you can read with precision and confidence, no memorization needed."
—NANCY HENDRICKSON, author of *Ancestral Tarot*, *Ancestral Grimoire*, and *Ancestral Séance*

"Tempest skillfully weaves the technical and approachable, spiritual and practical, hilarious and sincere, to create a vital, original, and enjoyable guide to the art of tarot reading."
—ENFYS J. BOOK, author of *Queer Rites*

"A potent and refreshing guide that invites readers to experience tarot as a full-body, intuitive practice. Blending art, movement, numerology, and personal insight, Zakroff offers a holistic approach that empowers both beginners and seasoned readers to connect deeply with their tarot cards, grounding the tarot beyond memorized meanings.... This book is an inspiring resource for anyone ready to make tarot their own."
—ETHONY DAWN, author of *Become an Exceptional Tarot Reader*

"Whether you're new to tarot or a seasoned reader, *Tarot by Tempest* offers up a complete, clear, and profoundly insightful system. It's a full vision that transforms tarot's centuries-old tradition from mysterious to logical and approachable. Even the math-averse will find magic in numbers here.... If you've ever found tarot intimidating, this is the guide that will shift everything."
—RISSA MILLER, historian and tasseographer

"Absolutely anyone of any skill level can benefit from Tempest's take on the Tarot! She delves into it all: shapes and symbols, colors, card composition, bringing movement into your interpretation...even how to read the cards for yourself and others (with FAQs). All in a richly illustrated, accessible

format with easy-to-understand explanations, *Tarot by Tempest* will enable you to feel more confident."
—**KAJIRA DJOUMAHNA,** artist and crone

"This book strips Tarot down to its bones and rebuilds it with numbers, symbols, and movement that make it fresh, sharp, and relevant. It's the kind of method you'll return to again and again, no matter how many decks or years you've been reading."
—**ERIKA ROBINSON,** author of *The Language of Lenormand*

"Tempest couldn't be a more appropriate moniker for Zakroff, their books, and their writing style. They are a force. This book is a shake-up and a game changer. It's a wild storm that stirs and breaks up a sea of monotonous, regurgitated information. It's the epitome of embodied. You are invited, required to utilize your mind, body, and soul while engaging with the lessons and tips. If you do that, if you show up for yourself and open your mind, Tarot becomes tangible. You will be a better reader for it, because of it.... What a fresh, new take on the system of Tarot."
—**JACLYN CHERIE,** owner of the Nephilim Rising, algorithm magick creator, folk herbalist, magickal consultant, ordained minister, word alchemist, Usui Reiki Master, and author and editor for Girl God Books

"Whether you are just starting out on the Fool's Journey or are a seasoned traveller, Zakroff breathes new life into the bones of Tarot by inviting the reader to explore a novel and engaging multisensory, five-dimensional interaction with the cards."
—**KENN PAYNE,** author of *Oracle of the Hekatean Path*

"Laura's unique voice and approach to Tarot, incorporating math (of all things) and movement, is something new and different. Having been a reader for 40 years, it is really hard for me to find something that fits that description.... Like all Laura's work, this book is a gift."
—**RAVEN MORGAINE,** author of *Yemaya: Orisha Goddess and Queen of the Sea*

"Dance the tarot? Math-infused magick? *Tarot by Tempest* takes on those seemingly quixotic quests and succeeds beautifully."
—**RICK DE YAMPERT,** author of *Crows and Ravens*

TAROT
by Tempest

© Carrie Meyer/Insomniac Studios

About the Author

Laura Tempest Zakroff (she/they) is a professional artist, author, performer, and Modern Traditional Witch based in New England. She holds a BFA from the Rhode Island School of Design, and her artwork has received awards and honors worldwide. Her work embodies myth and the esoteric through her drawings and paintings, jewelry, talismans, and other designs.

Laura is the author of several best-selling Llewellyn books, including *Weave the Liminal, Sigil Witchery, Visual Alchemy,* and *Anatomy of a Witch,* as well as the artist and author of the *Sigil Witchery Oracle, Anatomy of a Witch Oracle,* and *Liminal Spirits Oracle.* She edited *The New Aradia: A Witch's Handbook to Magical Resistance, The Gorgon's Guide to Magical Resistance,* and *Serpents of Circe: A Manual to Magical Resilience* from Revelore Press. Laura is the creative force behind several community events and teaches workshops online and worldwide. Find out more at www.lauratempestzakroff.com and https://linktr.ee/owlkeyme.

TAROT by Tempest

Playing with Numbers, Meaning & Movement

LAURA TEMPEST ZAKROFF

LLEWELLYN
WOODBURY, MINNESOTA

First Edition
First Printing, 2026

Book design by Donna Burch-Brown
Cover art by Laura Tempest Zakroff
Cover design by Kevin R. Brown
Interior art by Laura Tempest Zakroff
Tarot Original 1909 Deck © 2021 with art created by Pamela Colman Smith and Arthur Edward Waite. Used with permission of Lo Scarabeo.

Llewellyn Publications is a registered trademark of Llewellyn Worldwide Ltd.

Photography is used for illustrative purposes only. The persons depicted may not endorse or represent the book's subject.

Library of Congress Cataloging-in-Publication Data (Pending)
ISBN: 978-0-7387-7946-1

Llewellyn Publications
A Division of Llewellyn Worldwide Ltd.
2143 Wooddale Drive
Woodbury, MN 55125-2989
www.llewellyn.com

Printed in the United States of America

GPSR Representation:
UPI-2M PLUS d.o.o., Medulićeva 20, 10000 Zagreb, Croatia
matt.parsons@upi2mbooks.hr

Other Works by Laura Tempest Zakroff

Books & Oracles

Sigil Witchery Oracle
(Llewellyn, 2024)

Serpents of Circe: A Manual to Magical Resilience
(Coeditor, Revelore, 2024)

Visual Alchemy
(Llewellyn, 2022)

Anatomy of a Witch Oracle
(Llewellyn, 2022)

The Gorgon's Guide to Magical Resistance
(Editor, Revelore, 2022)

Anatomy of a Witch
(Llewellyn, 2021)

Liminal Spirits Oracle
(Llewellyn, 2020)

Weave the Liminal
(Llewellyn, 2019)

Sigil Witchery
(Llewellyn, 2018)

The Witch's Altar (with Jason Mankey)
(Llewellyn, 2018)

The New Aradia
(Editor, Revelore, 2018)

The Witch's Cauldron
(Llewellyn, 2017)

Coloring Books

Myth & Magick (2016)

The Art of Bellydance (2016)

Witch's Brew (2016)

Steampunk Menagerie (2015)

Instructional DVDs

DecoDance (2015)

Bellydance Artistry (2011)

Contributions

A Witch's Ally Oracle (by Dodie Graham McKay)
(Artist, Llewellyn, 2026)

Gemini Witch (by Ivo Dominguez, Jr.)
(Llewellyn, 2023)

Llewellyn's 2023 Magical Moon Calendar
(Artist, Llewellyn, 2023)

Llewellyn's Witches' Spell-A-Day Almanac
(Artist, Llewellyn, 2019–)

Witches & Pagans and *SageWoman* magazines
(Illustrator, BBI Media)

To Professor Robert Mathiesen—thank you for helping to reveal the Tarot and other occult mysteries to me with such kindness and consideration when I was just starting to figure all of this (and myself) out.

To the unsung heroes of metaphysical shops everywhere—those who create spaces for community to gather and for services like Tarot readings to take place—especially the employees who are on the front lines of assisting the general public every day, often wrangling both clients and readers alike. I see and appreciate you!

Contents

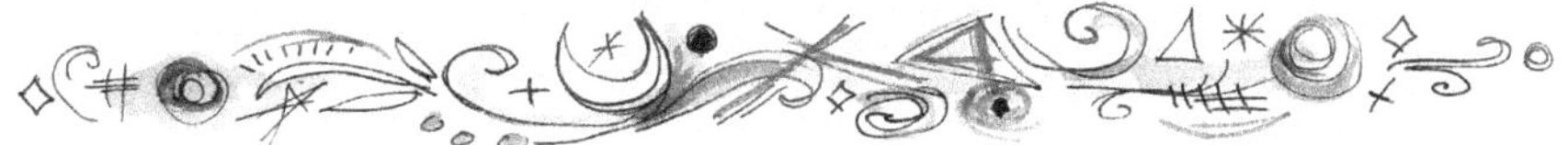

Introduction

Have you ever thought about what part of your body is used for divination? Where are psychic ability and intuition housed or do they originate from? How do you physically and mentally glean the answers to discover the meaning of cards laid out before you? Do you use your mind, your body, your spirit, or something else?

I believe the answer is all of the above and more. We use our hands to shuffle the deck and lay out spreads, our eyes to see the cards, our mind to remember, formulate, and decipher symbols and patterns, our spirit or proverbial gut to listen to what our intuition may offer, and our voice to speak the stories revealed by the cards. Our imagination allows us to both play and problem-solve as we consider the cards. We truly perceive with the whole of our being in order to interpret the cards before us.

That may seem like a whole lot of parts to get on board in order to become a proficient reader—and well, yes, technically it can be—but the journey doesn't have to be overly complicated or a massive ordeal. The process can actually be fun and enlightening and ultimately enhance the whole of your magical practice.

The pages ahead of you hold my multilayer approach to deepening your understanding of the Tarot. The techniques will fascinate your mind, inspire your heart, and be felt in your bones. You'll not only be able to read the cards more quickly and summon their meaning but also learn to recognize how the cards are speaking to you on an emotional and a spiritual level—and unlock parts of your unconscious understanding through movement.

I know that sounds very metaphysical and lovely, but what on earth does that mean in practical terms?

Well, what if I told you there's a way you can learn to effectively read the Tarot without memorizing every single card beforehand? And that, using this method, you would be able to pick up almost any Tarot deck—including one you've never seen before—and be able to give an accurate reading?

Not only that, but you can also use this same method to dive deeper into your decks and train your brain to recognize how symbols, colors, and visual composition reveal the story of each card. Elemental correlations will take on new meaning and movement in how they bring energy to the Tarot. You'll be more conscious of the patterns inherent in the cards and how they can interact with each other. This approach brings the cards to life in new ways.

Lastly, this method can also guide your body to explore even deeper meaning within the cards and connect with your intuition at a core, primal level. Your body can be your most primary magical tool, regardless of your age, size, or physical ability. The mysteries that life dances are stored within your own blood, breath, and bone—and they can be revealed through movement.

What is this Witchcraft, you ask? It's the magic that happens when we combine practices rooted in math, art, and movement.

What? Math? Art? And DANCE? Yes, I'm well aware that each one of these words by itself can summon some uncomfortable feelings for a lot of adults when presented with the possible task of having to draw, move their bodies, or do some calculations on the spot. And here I am mentioning a possibly terrifying trinity of all three combined. I understand the discomfort and even fear that may arise due to past bad experiences. But I promise that it's worth the work.

I've come to realize that both my calling and one of my apparent superpowers in this life is getting folks on board with ideas that are not as scary as social programming would have us believe.[1] Math doesn't have to be complicated, art isn't just for gallery walls, and moving your body doesn't require choreography or a sweat-worthy workout. I believe in accessibility and demystification—as well as recognizing that our brains and bodies respond to a wide range of stimuli for effective learning.

It doesn't matter how many times I've taught classes and workshops, I am endlessly delighted by the feedback from folks that my approach excites and inspires them. That's why I do the work I do. So many people have told me after taking my Tarot workshops that "I've been reading for decades and you taught me a whole new way of looking at the cards that is exciting and fresh." Others have confided to me, "I always hated math, and you just opened up the cards AND MATH to me in ways I didn't think possible." I've had folks confess they were really scared to take one of my Sigil Witchery classes because they are decidedly "not an artist," and those same individuals still send me photos of the art they're making now. I've had countless participants nervously eye the door for their escape route when I mention dance in a class or ritual, and they're always the ones sharing with me that they didn't know how badly they needed to move. It's important to me to help folks overcome their fears, to realize there isn't just one way to do the thing, and to assure them that they're in a safe place to explore new things. I feel this way because I have been there myself and I want others to have the opportunity to enjoy the process—which means I know you can do the thing!

I invite you to come on a journey that can help revolutionize how you look at the Tarot and your own magical practice.

What You Can Expect to Learn from This Book

This book explores my unique approach to reading the Tarot, which I have developed over the last twenty-five-plus years. It is the culmination of the work I have done as an artist, a writer, a Witch, a dancer, and a performer—

1. My other superpower is being able to tell if a lead singer of a band is a jerk or not depending on their vocals. It's actually more handy than you might expect if you're in the music scene, but also kind of a bummer.

filtered through my neurospicy brain. My background, observations, and experiences as an artist and a dancer have deeply influenced and informed how I use numbers and shapes and combine them with symbolism and meanings. I am a Witch who loves the Tarot. I am constantly curious about the correlations and patterns present in our lives and why we do what we do. And as a Gemini, OMG I love sharing helpful information with others. My hope and focus is to make this method available as an accessible format for a wide range of folks and experience levels.

Here are some of the goals I have for you:

- Learn an accessible and easy-to-remember way to read the Tarot without memorizing the little white book (LWB).
- Acquire the ability to pick up nearly any deck (or even playing cards) and read effectively without having studied the deck in depth.
- Build your confidence as a reader and learn to be guided by your intuition with a solid foundation.
- Form skills for better observation and pattern recognition.
- Enhance and empower your ability to decipher meaning from symbols, colors, shapes, composition, and other imagery.
- Discover new ideas for designing your own spreads and using established spreads.
- Consider innovative ways to build meditations and personal practices using the cards with math.
- Learn to embody magic accessibly and creatively while uncovering meaning in movement—and, let's face it, we could all use a little more movement in our modern lives!

I am also including some Tarot basics in case you are fairly new in your own Tarot journey. My hope is that with this book, I'm providing insight to both new and seasoned readers alike. If you consider yourself an old pro, please keep in mind that not everything in this book is directed at you. But brushing up on the basics doesn't hurt—especially if you're going to be instructing others at some point. I find that it always helps to see how others cover the basics in genres I am already familiar with, as there's the potential for seeing something I know in a new way. For the newbies, some ideas may initially go over your head, but please remember that we can only absorb so much material at once. I find that we recognize and respond to the material that we need to in the moment—and the rest you will become aware of once you've gained more experience.

Hopefully you understand that I'm not going to be asking you to do advanced algebra or calculus here, but rather I'm opening the doors to a process that is actually rather fun and can enhance your entire magical practice in new ways. We will be looking at the symbolism of the numbers and discovering the energetic motion and shapes they can embody. We will be enlisting the simple applications of addition, subtraction, division, and multiplication. These processes can lend insight not only to how you interpret spreads but also to how you can connect more deeply with the cards themselves.

The numbers we will explore together are a guide to the energy of the Tarot. They will give you a solid foundation to build upon. At a glance, you will be able to get a quick yet fairly accurate overview of what you're looking at. You will be able to assess the numbers set before you and get a sense of the story happening in the cards. Then you can use your intuitive impressions of the images, symbols, and colors to glean more information that is specific to the situation. You can also tap into spiritual connection for additional messages, which means consulting with spirits, ancestors, etc., if that is part of your practice.

By the end of this book, I hope you will also find a new appreciation for math, an affinity for art, and an enthusiasm for movement exploration—and, of course, get a lot more out of your Tarot readings!

My Tarot Journey

Before we truly begin, I feel it's important to share with you how I got into reading Tarot. This background will give some context to how I developed my approach and fine-tuned it over the years.

My journey with the Tarot began when I was eighteen and someone gifted me a copy of Legend: The Arthurian Tarot from Llewellyn. I immediately dove into uncovering the symbolism, learning how to read for myself and others as well as thinking about making my own decks (as one does when one is a young artist going to art school and full of vigor—and a bit of a habitual overachiever.

As it happened, I was also taking a liberal arts class that centered on Arthurian romances. As part of the curriculum, we read *Sir Gawain and the Green Knight*, Malory's *Le Morte d'Arthur*, Tennyson's *Idylls of the King*, and Spenser's *The Faerie Queene*. These fascinating texts gave me another level of mythology to merge with my Tarot deck, as the cards referenced figures and situations from those tales. The Arthurian stories helped to illuminate what I saw in the cards. I recognized that, despite the age of these myths and their often archaic language,[2] human nature has common themes that we all tend to experience in one way or another.

I decided to try this experiment for myself. I created a Major Arcana–only deck based on Tennyson's poem "The Lady of Shalott," using hand-pulled etchings to create the cards. I went through the poem and pulled out lines that I felt connected best with each trump card, illustrated them, and then made a folded booklet of the whole poem to accompany it. Both the deck and the booklet printed all on one large plate—very much like how modern decks are printed on one sheet and then cut. I carved and block printed a stamp on the back of each card and even hand-made boxes and bags for each deck!

But let's back this train up a bit. Before I got serious about making art involving the Tarot, I first worked on learning how to read my deck. After familiarizing myself with the cards and the little white book, I practiced reading online for folks I encountered on IRC.[3] They would type out a question and I would shuffle and pull some cards. Since I was just starting

2. I did get to add *smote* to my vocabulary, a definite bonus to working through Middle English texts.

3. Internet Relay Chat—basically a digital grandparent of today's Discord. Same core idea, but without any graphics. This was in the time before emojis or being able to post photos, animated GIFs, memes, etc.

out, I would first follow my intuition to see what the cards were saying and then check the LWB to see if there was anything else I should know about the cards. Then I would type up the response and send that to the person. It was a low-stress situation since I wasn't face-to-face with anyone, but I was still surprised to get consistent feedback that I was spot-on with my readings.

The Lady of Shalott Tarot Created by the Author in the Late '90s

I also learned some tips from one of my college professors about non-traditional spreads and other ways to further develop my intuition and understanding of the cards. Thanks to his guidance, I developed my go-to spread and several related variations on it, which you'll learn about in chapter 7. This step was so important for me, as I wasn't a fan of the Celtic Cross spread—which seemed to be included with the instructions of every Tarot deck at that time. I needed something that gelled better with my brain and gave me a sense of time and movement in the spread.

Soon I started offering readings on my lunch breaks. I worked at the RISD Store (an art supply / college bookstore), and on nice summer days I would go outside and sit at one of the picnic benches along the downtown waterfront with my cards and a little painted wooden sign, which I still have today!

Hand-Painted Sign by the Author

This situation not only brought in a little extra money with tips but also gave me experience reading for a more diverse group of people face-to-face. I soon started reading at local metaphysical shops on evenings and weekends. I also began doing psychic fairs that were within an hour's drive of where I lived, often doing readings as well as vending my artwork.

When I moved to the Bay Area in California a year after graduating from RISD, I thought I'd go to work at a gallery (which was what I had been doing in Rhode Island shortly after graduation) or, even better, a museum. However, a few days after arriving in the South Bay, I happened upon one of the largest metaphysical stores I'd ever seen. It was called the

Psychic Eye and was part of a small chain of stores located throughout California and Nevada. The shop had anywhere from four to eight psychic readers on the schedule at any given time. I figured picking up a reading gig was worth a shot while I sorted out getting an art job.

I had to give a reading to the store manager as an interview, which was probably the most nervous I've ever been to give someone a reading. The manager was an imposing person, both gruff and guarded energetically. But I pulled my shit together, gave them a reading, and was hired on the spot! On my first day on the job, I was introduced trial-by-fire style to doing phone readings. No one had mentioned this delivery system was a thing I'd be doing when I interviewed for the job,[4] but it ended up being not that much different from doing readings on IRC—except, of course, it was more immediate. Instead of typing, I needed to talk through the cards and be a careful listener. Pretty soon I was very much in demand, often doing anywhere from six to eight readings a day, depending on the length of the reading.

Over the next three years, I'd end up providing over three thousand readings, according to the daily record book I kept. As we were situated in Silicon Valley, I read for an incredible assortment of people, especially those in the tech industry, and people from every background you can imagine. And with phone readings, people called in from all over the world. I learned a whole lot about both people and Tarot reading during those few years. Occasionally a phone client would make an appearance in the shop to get a reading in person. They were often surprised to find that I was a young twenty-something person versus someone much older, like they pictured me to be,[5] partly because of the context and depth of the readings I gave them and partly because I developed a soothing phone voice for the job.

4. This is probably part of the reason why I greatly dislike talking on the phone today with strangers.

5. This was the early days of the internet, so there weren't bios or photos of the readers on a website. People would call to book a reading and the front-of-store folks would tell them who was available and maybe a little bit about us. That was all they had to go on.

Then one day the shop closed rather unexpectedly. (This is where some may want to make a joke about psychics not seeing that coming—but the hilarious thing is that I *did* have a dream just beforehand! Oh, that one anxiety dream was supposed to actually mean something??) The abrupt closure turned out to be a very good thing for me personally, as doing readings full-time took up a lot of my focus and energy. I quickly pivoted and found a smaller local shop to do readings at occasionally for my regular clients. I also switched to an arts-based job for my main work. My visual art and dancing careers blossomed, as I had more energy and brainpower to devote to them.

In the years that followed, I would offer readings less and less as a professional service. It eventually got to the point where I would just do readings for friends and family who needed them—and, of course, for myself. However, my love for the Tarot has remained and continues to be a major influence on my work and my spiritual practice. In my book *Anatomy of a Witch: A Map to the Magical Body*, the reader journeys through the first ten cards of the Major Arcana as they work through the material. Every Winter Solstice on my Patreon, we pull thirteen cards for the year to come, one for each month and one overall.

During the COVID-19 pandemic when everything was happening strictly online, I began offering "Tempest's Tips for Tarot," which is a class I started teaching way back when I was reading at the Psychic Eye in the Bay Area. I was surprised by the enthusiastic response to my approach, especially from folks who had been reading as long as I had or longer. When things opened back up for in-person events, I was invited to teach at Witch City Tarot Gathering in Salem, Massachusetts. I decided to test the waters with a sampling of the very material you are holding right now. The response was phenomenal—I had expected to be run out of the room for heresy, but instead I received a standing ovation! I tested it again in a shorter format for the Northwest Tarot Symposium (NWTS) in Portland, Oregon, that fall. The attendees at NWTS were a different crowd from those at the Witch City event in many ways, but the response to my class was similar. And so now, nearly thirty years of my Tarot experience has found its way into book format, with the hope of inspiring and aiding more people on their own Tarot journey.

Of course, there's probably one burning question you're wondering about if you're familiar with my work: Why haven't I made a whole Tarot deck yet? After all, I've created and published several popular oracle decks. Well, I have brainstormed many a Tarot deck over the years—easily over a dozen different concepts. But for me, it's one thing to create my own system from scratch (such as my oracles) and another to pay homage to an established system while also having the stamina to do artwork for 78 cards. I know that might seem silly, because I've done numerous oracle decks now with anywhere from 42 to 60 cards each. I guess it comes down to settling on the right idea that I feel both pays respect to Tarot and integrates my own unique voice into the format. Really, it's just a matter of time, so depending on when you're reading this book, this whole paragraph will likely have become moot.

Decades after getting my first deck, the Tarot is still a major influence on my work and my spiritual practice. The Tarot has been a constant companion and guide—and I'm excited to share what I've learned along the way with you!

Now let's get shuffling!

CHAPTER 1
Meet the Tarot

If you are new to Tarot, I want to make sure you have a good understanding of the basics before moving forward. If you consider yourself intermediate to advanced, it doesn't hurt to get a quick refresher, especially if you're introducing others to the Tarot.

What is the Tarot essentially? Tarot is a card-based tool used for divination. Methods of divination that use paper cards fall under the category of cartomancy. The Tarot not only can help us look into the future but can also reveal the present and the past. It may seem odd in the context of "fortune-telling" to note that the past and the present are just as important as the future, but we often miss big clues in our own lives. The Tarot gives us insight into the patterns that surround us and the choices we have or can make—or have made.

The exact origins of the Tarot are unknown and fakelore abounds about where it came from. The Tarot is a culmination of many roots and is actively used by a wide array of people from all over the world. Educated theories from historians suggest that the earliest roots come from Arabic and/or Chinese card games printed on paper. We know that the closest versions of what we see today emerged from mid-fifteenth-century decks originating in Italy that later spread throughout Europe. These cards were developed further by artists and occultists in France, Germany, England, and far beyond.[6] Whole books have been written on the history of the Tarot and who has used it, so I will point you to the "Suggested Resources" section at the end of the book for further exploration. A word of caution

6. Kaplan, *The Encyclopedia of Tarot, Volume 1*, 23.

about online information: Be wary of the hot takes that regularly cycle through the interwebs, sparking controversy without much basis in fact.

The Tarot traditionally consists of 78 cards, of which there are 22 Major Arcana cards and 56 Minor Arcana cards. I say "traditionally" in reference to the standard number of cards for Tarot decks published in the last two centuries, particularly the Rider-Waite-Smith (RWS), the Tarot of Marseilles, and the Thoth deck—and all decks that are inspired by those three.

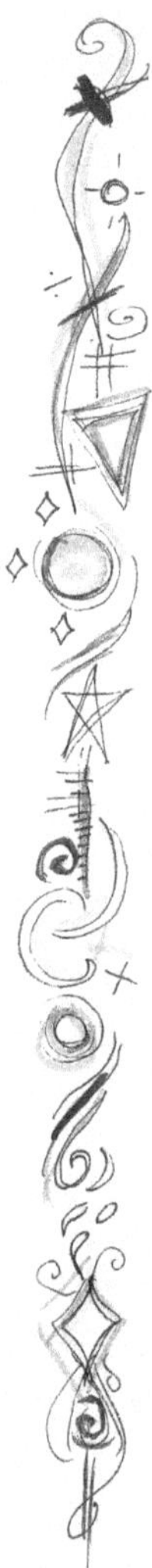

A Quick Look at the Big Three

The Rider-Waite-Smith (RWS) Tarot is one of the most popular, widely available decks. It was created through the joint efforts of two members of the Hermetic Order of the Golden Dawn—written by A. E. Waite and illustrated by Pamela Colman Smith—and was published by William Rider & Son in 1909. Initially it was referred to as the Rider-Waite Tarot, but "Smith" was more recently added to give proper credit to the artist. As Rider is no longer the publisher, many enthusiasts now refer to the deck as the Smith-Waite.

The Thoth Tarot was painted by Frieda Harris with direction from Aleister Crowley. Crowley's *The Book of Thoth* was published in 1944 and serves as a basis for the deck, but the actual deck wouldn't be published until 1967 by Llewellyn, years after both Harris and Crowley had passed. The Thoth deck utilizes several titles for the cards that differ from those in the RWS, adds additional symbolism and systems, and uses keywords, and some of the number associations are altered as well.

The Tarot of Marseille is a French interpretation of historical Italian Tarot decks that were popular in the seventeenth and eighteenth centuries. The first modern Tarot de Marseille was printed by Pierre Madenie of Dijon in 1709. The art on the cards of the Minor Arcana more closely resembles that of traditional playing cards than the pictorial representations we see in the RWS and Thoth.

The 22 Major Arcana cards emphasize the greater mysteries of life. They can be viewed as a journey or parts of a cycle, starting with the Fool. These cards describe big ideas, concepts, and themes happening in the querent's life. Think large paint strokes to get a feel for the setting or situation. They are the drumbeats that drive the song of life.

The 56 Minor Arcana cards guide us through the little mysteries. These cards point out the details that help define our journey, made up of the fine lines and sketches that help describe those details. They are the melodic instrumentation that builds on the rhythm set by the Major Arcana. Think of the Minor Arcana as the equivalent of the guitar, the violin, or the wind instruments that help tell the story and bring us in deeper. The Minor Arcana is made up of four suits, typically some variation of Wands, Swords, Cups, and Pentacles. These correspond to the four suits of playing cards: Clubs, Swords, Hearts, and Diamonds. Each suit has Ace through Ten and then four court cards (traditionally Page, Knight, Queen, and King). Each of the four suits typically has an elemental correspondence (Earth, Air, Fire, Water) as well, which adds another layer of meaning and insight. We will dive deeper into elemental correspondences and variations in chapter 5.

You may find decks that include additional trump cards that have been included to fit the creator's vision or to offer alternatives. An example would be decks that include multiple Lovers cards—featuring a woman and a man, two women, two men, or two folks outside of the gender binary. Depending on the querent, the reader can choose the card that fits the situation more appropriately. It behooves you to be aware of extra cards outside of the standard 78 before you start working with the deck so you understand whether or not you want to include them in your readings.

Some people ask why there are so many decks. Why do people keep revisiting the Tarot and adding their own take to it? Well, I believe there are so many ways to see life and be inspired, and the Tarot provides an excellent foundation for exploration. It's also important to keep in mind that the Tarot is an ever-evolving system. Over the centuries we've seen changing names and shifting meanings, as well as many approaches to illustrating the cards, how many cards are included, and even how they're used. In another fifty to a hundred years, Tarot enthusiasts may be pointing to some of our modern-day decks as historical offshoots of diversion from the proverbial Tarot tree in new directions.

Choosing a Tarot Deck

At this point in the timeline, there are thousands of Tarot decks out there to consider. The choice can be overwhelming, especially if you search online or simply see a full shelf of decks in a store. There's a theme deck for almost anything you can think of and probably some things you haven't. This cornucopia of cartomancy doesn't mean that every deck is thoughtfully designed and well crafted or will be a good fit for you. So how do you choose?

Sometimes what is locally available to you might be a pretty slim selection, depending on a shop's inventory and personal preferences. For those with choice paralysis, this minimizing of the options can be a good thing. There are some shops that specialize in stocking decks, and they might have hundreds to choose from. A lot of shops offer sample decks of what they have for sale so you can flip through the cards and get a feel for them in your hands before deciding. If they don't, search for the deck on YouTube and you'll likely find that some helpful person has made a flip-through video showcasing all the cards in the deck. Or you might find a website that shows some of the cards (like www.aeclectic.net). If you like what you see, you can pick up the deck right there on the spot and support your local business—which is awesome! You might even be able to buy the deck directly from the creator as well. If you're buying a deck online, just make sure it is from a reputable site, as there are plenty of sites peddling poor-quality knock-off decks.

What Do You Want in a Deck?

For me, the biggest thing is that the artwork must be pleasing to my eye—not just a few cards but the vast majority. This is why being able to flip through a deck or see all the cards in a video is helpful, as publishers tend to highlight some of the best cards and the rest may not be as successful visually. Another thing to consider is whether I like how both the Major and the Minor Arcana have been illustrated. Can I easily tell the cards apart and read any necessary text or numbers? Some decks don't have very legible fonts or the symbols used to represent the suits may be hard to decipher. If there's a border, does it distract from or enhance the art?

Moving from visual to technical details, I evaluate how the cards fit and feel in my hands. Are they easy for me to shuffle? Is the cardstock too thick or too thin? Does the paper texture obscure or enhance the look and feel of the cards?

One of the most crucial things overall is that when I look at the cards, are they talking to me or feeling chatty? You might be wondering what the heck I mean by that. No, the cards aren't physically talking to me.[7] I'm referring to a sensation that's part intuitive feeling and part discernment. I get the sense that the deck is telling me a story and wants to engage with me. Some decks are very beautiful, yet they feel devoid of that vital spark. Something I may not instantly click with on an aesthetic level could be very interesting to read with nonetheless. Every deck has a personality, so see what gels with yours!

What to Look Out For

Here is a list of things to consider or be aware of when selecting a deck.

Representation: Do you find yourself being visually or conceptually represented in the cards? Traditional (and even some modern) decks can be very cisgendered, white, and heteronormative in their presentation. Do you see yourself reflected in the skin colors, body types, ages, gender expressions, and sexuality shown by the deck? The great news is that newer, more diverse decks are coming out daily, so there are definitely some excellent choices out there. Also, consider who your target audience or querents may be if you're reading for other people. Will they

7. But I do suspect it's only a matter of time before someone makes a deck with microchips in the cards or a QR code you scan for the cards to speak or to project a hologram that explains your selection.

also see themselves in the cards? Some people solve this conundrum by selecting a deck that's more fantastical, featuring plants or animals instead of humans, abstract designs, or otherworldly imagery. Find a balance between what inspires and connects with you and what may click with your querents.

A Perfect Fit and Feel: Get a deck that fits comfortably in your hands, so it's easy to shuffle and work with. There are also many cardstocks and paperweights as well as textures and finishes out there. Thick cards look beautiful and feel sturdy, but they can be really hard to shuffle and may even slice up your hands. Thin cards can damage easily. Some people love a linen texture because they say it's easier to shuffle. I prefer a smooth surface because I think the linen pattern interrupts the artwork, especially when there's a lot of fine detail. Foil edging is gorgeous, but it can wear off on your hands with use. It can take a while to figure out what the perfect combination is for you when it comes to size and finish. If you can, definitcly see if you can try a sample of the deck that visually appeals to you so you know the size and feel also work.

The Whole Deal: Make sure it's a complete Tarot deck with 78 cards. Some artist explorations contain only the Major Arcana. These are handy for certain exercises and exploration, but if you think you're getting a full deck for the price and it's just a partial one, disappointment is on the immediate horizon. Read product descriptions carefully!

Which of the Big Three? As discussed earlier, the most common kinds of Tarot decks fall in one of three categories: the Rider-Waite-Smith Tarot, which most newer decks are based on or inspired by; the Tarot of Marseille, where the Minor Arcana cards are most akin to playing cards in visual presentation, as they have an antique look to them; and the Thoth Tarot. What we will cover in this book can be applied to all three, but there are differences that are particular to each deck. I typically recommend a RWS deck variation when starting out—but that doesn't mean you have to use the version you see in this book or a similar one. As I mentioned in the introduction, I started with Legend: The Arthurian

Tarot, which is based on the RWS but looks completely different visually. Go with what calls to you. That's what's most important here.

Tarot Is Tarot Is Tarot: Don't confuse an oracle deck for a Tarot deck. Oracle cards are their own systems and absolutely have their uses, but they're not the same as the Tarot. People tend to use these terms interchangeably all the time, causing even more confusion. Tarots are technically cartomancy oracles, but not all oracles are Tarot. Lenormand is another cartomancy system that is similar to the Tarot, but again is its own animal.

The Real Deal: Avoid purchasing a knock-off deck. These are fairly easy to spot in person because they often sport a QR code on the box instead of containing the actual booklet (despite what the box says). Watch for not only a QR code but also flimsy slipcover boxes and bad shrink-wrap. These decks are rarely the same size as the originals, are poorly manufactured, and are ripping off artists and authors in your community. They may be cheaper, but do you really want to read with a deck that's been made with such bad intent?

Support Human Creators: Similar to knowing where a deck legitimately comes from is the issue of AI-generated Tarot decks. Please note that I am talking about decks that are created by feeding prompts into a computer versus digitally designed art created by an artist. As both an artist and an author, I am very much not a fan of AI-generated work, though I understand why some artists may use it. From an intellectual and artistic copyright standpoint, my own work has been pirated to generate such works, and that's bullshit. As a Tarot reader, I find AI-generated decks on the whole—besides being ethically dubious—to be lackluster and derivative. Why? In many cases, most if not all of the visual and symbolic design choices and decisions are not being made by a human being, with purpose and clarity. It may take more time to generate each image from scratch, whether by traditional media or digitally painted, but I believe the result is far more potent. Most publishers are avoiding AI-generated decks because of the copyright issues, but you might come across some indie decks that are elusive in their language about how the deck was created. (End soapbox scene.)

You may have heard the "lore" that you cannot purchase your own deck—that it must be gifted. This "wisdom" makes the rounds online every few years and sometimes even shows up in books. Whether this fakelore is the product of gatekeeping (someone trying to curb others from trying the Tarot for themselves) or misplaced mysticism, it's pure nonsense. While I will say it is certainly nice to be gifted a deck, you can absolutely buy your own. Just ask me about the obscene number of decks my partner and I have collected over the years.[8]

Again, I know it's easy to be overwhelmed with all these choices, but do allow yourself to start somewhere. I tend to be of the mind that whatever deck you start with—however it comes to you—is the right one to set you on your Tarot path. If after a while a deck doesn't seem like the right fit for you anymore, you can always trade, sell, or gift it to someone else,[9] or maybe just put it aside for a while and explore whatever else comes your way! You're not signing a blood oath to work with one deck to rule them all—or at least you shouldn't be!

Getting Acquainted

Before you begin to actively use a new deck, I recommend taking some time to connect with it and get a feel for the cards. I call this practice "attuning to the deck," and it helps to build a relationship with your chosen tool. Think of attuning like this: If you're going to spend a lot of time with someone, asking intimate questions, it's best to get to know their name, preferences, and personality quirks.

Start by flipping through the cards, looking at each image briefly until you've gone through the whole deck. (Later you can do daily pulls to familiarize yourself with each card one at a time, discovering each card more intimately.) Next, shuffle the deck for a bit to get a feel for it in your hands.

8. We don't have a Tarot problem. I like to think of it as a Tarot solution.

9. Tarot swaps are a lot of fun at conventions and festivals, and since the decks are almost always open, you can check them out first!

When you're done, you can wrap it firmly in a cloth or place it in a sturdy bag that matches the feel of your deck. You can use the original box the deck came in as well, depending on the durability of the box. A lot of newer decks have very sturdy boxes that are quite nice, but some still come in slipcases or tuck boxes that are a pain in the ass to get the deck in and out of easily—and offer little protection. Or they come in oversize boxes that are difficult to easily transport.

I find it's best to transfer the deck to an easy-to-carry zipper pouch or drawstring bag. My primary reading deck is also wrapped in a larger reading cloth and placed inside a bag, so I just need to grab the bag and go. A protective bag is often the easiest to travel with. If you find yourself acquiring multiple decks and placing them in bags, I recommend adding a tag to the outside (to the zipper pull or string) and labeling which deck it is. You think you will remember what deck is in there, but chances are good that you won't.

Travel Tip: If you plan to do a lot of traveling with your deck, I highly recommend placing your bag or box in a ziplock or similar waterproof bag. You never know when rain, spilled coffee, wine, etc. is coming for your pocket, backpack, purse, or luggage, especially if you're going camping. You'll thank me later.

If you can, carry the wrapped deck on your person (in a purse or backpack or coat pocket) when you go out into the world. For at least three nights, sleep with the deck under your pillow or bed or place it somewhere nearby. You can also place the deck on your altar if you have one. The idea is that you're establishing a connection with the deck to the rhythm of your life.

You may also want to get a little notebook that will fit in your Tarot bag. This notebook acts as a mini journal where you can keep track of daily pulls, insights, and other thoughts. I recommend starting a daily practice where you shuffle and pull a single card for yourself. A good time to do your pull is either first thing in the morning as you start your day or as you're winding down for the night. Write down your impressions of the card and anything else that comes to you. How does it make you feel? What do you notice about it? Then—and only after you've worked your own intuition—you can refer to the booklet and compare notes. Add any additional information you discovered that feels relevant to your little journal. If you do this on a daily or at least semi-regular basis, you'll become much more familiar with your deck quickly. The act of writing down your thoughts also aids in building memory, so you're more likely to remember this information in the future!

By the way, if you keep pulling the same card, make a note of that too, then pull an additional card to examine why it keeps coming up. The deck is definitely sharing a message with you about that card, which is why I think it's key to recognize the frequency of the card. But when you're starting out and getting to know a deck, it's best to make sure you're meeting the other cards too, despite what the deck insists upon.

Most importantly, play, practice, and learn to trust your intuition.

CHAPTER 2
The Magic of Numbers, Meaning & Movement

In this chapter we will explore the roots of my method—how math, art, and movement can assist the process of unlocking the mysteries of the Tarot. First we will clear away misconceptions so there's room to explore without fear or anxiety. Then we will investigate how each of these three subjects has a vital role to play.

Rethinking Our Feelings About Math, Art, and Movement

Our society likes to propagate the idea that math is hard, scary, or not terribly useful in the "real world." People tend to think that math only has to do with exact sciences and applied practices such as chemistry, engineering, and architecture. But we're surrounded by math in so many ways that don't require a college degree or advanced calculations to appreciate. Nor is math relegated only to paying bills and balancing your bank accounts. Math is truly so much more than lines and numbers in textbooks and complex equations, something complicated that may induce a headache or make us feel vulnerable or not smart enough to accomplish a task.

When we are considering the odds of something happening, such as whether we will win a game, hit traffic driving to that event, or get stuck in a downpour, we're using our knowledge of probability and statistics. In the kitchen, when we need to halve or double a recipe, we're using division and multiplication. When it's time to germinate seeds for the garden, we estimate how many of the seeds will sprout, then we often have to reduce the number by thinning the extras so the best will thrive. Then when we're ready to put plants in the ground, we need to consider how many hours of sunlight is optimal, as well as how much growth space we should plan for so the plants will thrive. Picture framing may seem like just throwing some art or a photo behind glass, but there's careful measuring required, plus adding up fractions for wood and glass allowance and figuring out how best to conserve expensive material—and what to do if you mess up! When we select furniture for a room, we are working with the geometry of a space: figuring out how much room is needed, what the flow will be like, and how it will best accommodate our daily living needs. If you're mixing incense or creating anointing oils, you must consider ratios and ingredient amounts to make the specific end result you desire—and keep a record of it so you can repeat your results! In so many ways, we can see that math is essential for problem-solving and helps us navigate through life, even if the equations aren't always obvious.

Let's also recognize the social optics: Math is generally not considered "cool" in school. I remember being teased in grade school that, because I did well in math, I "liked" it. (Imagine "liked" being said with all the smug, singsongy snideness of a petulant fourth grader.) This correlation was somehow something shameful in the eyes of my peers. On top of all the *other* reasons I didn't fit in, doing well at math was just one more stick on the looming pyre stack of social anathema. No amount of crying "But I don't *like* math!" would have made a difference anyway.

Honestly, though, I didn't actually like math back then. But as a kid, I was a neurospicy overachiever who internalized that I must get good grades in everything, so getting less than a B in *anything* was out of the question. I also didn't understand much of math as it was presented in school, which was incredibly frustrating. For me to understand what was being presented, I had to find another way to look at formulas, equations, and systems to have any of those lessons make sense. Insight often came from a whole other field of study or subject matter, such as art or biology.

I often took a much longer road to get back to a concept,[10] but I typically had a better understanding of what I was trying to figure out in the end.

But now, what do I think about it as an adult? Math is totally magic and I derive great glee from recognizing and utilizing it in my work. It's become a kind of game! I see all the ways that shapes, numbers, probabilities, and patterns play a role in how I perceive the world. I often muse about the question "What if math and magic were taught alongside each other in school?" If that were the case, I think we'd be a lot freer in embracing and sustaining our innate creativity, as well as be more skilled in comprehension, critical thinking, and communication—all abilities that can help lead to a more equitable, creative, and compassionate society.

How? Well, that brings us to our next danger topic: art. Art may not have the popularity issues that math contends with, but society sure has a lot of ideas regarding art that just aren't healthy. You may have heard some of them: that art isn't important to culture, that making art is frivolous, that art is expensive and only for the elite. The reality is that art is vital to culture, making art is essential and necessary, and art is (and should be) accessible to all.

Human civilization happened because of art, not the other way around. Starting back at the moment when our ancestors in the caves used their hands to apply pigments to the stone walls, art changed how we perceived ourselves and the world around us. As we drew animals and shapes, we learned to focus our attention, studying the world around us in greater detail while expanding our capacity and ability to use our memories. Art served as a means to communicate with each other as well as the unseen forces in the world around us. We also learned to create symbols to simplify complex ideas. Art fostered our imagination and expanded our forms of expression. We developed creative intelligence to be able to solve problems in new ways and develop new ideas.

10. Spoiler alert: If you haven't read my other books, such as *Sigil Witchery* and *Weave the Liminal*, then you probably don't know that going the long way around paired with my eternal quest to find the *how* and the *why* something is done is basically the cornerstone of my signature innovations in magical practice. I'm weird, but it works.

For all these reasons and more, the making of art is valuable for our brains. Not only does art deepen our intelligence and general understanding of the world around us, but it also helps us express ourselves. We can explore our emotions, play with ideas, and engage in conversations with others about our experiences. Art builds empathy, strengthens imagination, creates community through engagement, and helps us sort out what's going on in our heads.

If you're making art, you're an artist. You may not see yourself as an "Artist" whose work is going to hang in a gallery or museum and garner all the money, but that's not what art-making is truly about anyway. Art is for everyone, both the creating and the viewing of it. Art doesn't have to be expensive, made with fancy materials—the main cost of art is the time we devote to the process. And as we can see from the benefits above, the wins far outweigh the sacrifice of time and effort in so many ways.

Art is also magic. Magic begins with thought, and art is a way to give shape, form, color, and direction to those thoughts. Images tell a story, all the while giving a tangible form to the possibilities found within our imagination.

I think the fear that most people have about art is that subconsciously they know art is about expression and they fear being exposed and vulnerable if they share that expression with the world. They fear that they will be judged for not being good enough, laughed at for their ideas, or dismissed. It's hard to be vulnerable, but I think it's harder not to have an accessible outlet to explore what's going on inside yourself. Not every work of art is going to be successful as a museum masterpiece, but every piece of art attempted is a successful exploration in its own right. Art is worth the effort.

Now where do math and art meet? When it comes to visual art, geometry plays a huge role in building form, designing composition, and building perspective. We divide a canvas into thirds to figure out where to best place the focal point and draw the viewer's eye around the work. We use formulas to figure out how to mix paints and glazes and charts to determine firing and drying times. When it comes to the performing arts, we also find that music, writing, dance, and many other forms of human expression rely on math for structure, from scales and patterns to sentence structures and choreography. In a musical scale, the intervals are based on rational frequency ratios or fractions to determine where notes land. Many poems and prose use a defined meter to set the rhythm quality and cadence, by using either a certain number of lines in a stanza or a single line containing a specific number of syllables, like the haiku's 5-7-5 structure. A choreography breaks down a song by time, rhythm, and melody while playing with the area of a stage and the shape dancers' bodies can create on top of it.

That brings us to our last bombshell: dance and movement. Whereas people fear their ideas being mocked or exposed through visual art, I find that most people's fears about dance center around their bodies. I have lost count of the number of times someone has said to me, "Oh, I would love to take a dance class, but I need to lose weight first." My advice: DANCE NOW. People also think you have to be graceful to dance. Well, I'm straight up going to share this truth with you: I may look graceful on stage, but in regular life I am a klutz. I can trip over nothing, hit my head on doorknobs, and collide with things in the shower. I wish I could maintain better body awareness at all times like I do on stage, but I'm human, nearsighted, and easily distracted by cats.

You don't move your body to be graceful; you move your body to live. As long as you are alive, everything *within you* is in motion, starting at the cellular level. When we focus our breath, consider the ebb and flow of our blood, hear the rhythm of our heartbeat, and engage our muscular and skeletal structure, we are beings of dance inside and out. Movement doesn't have to be a set of perfectly executed moves that create a complex choreography. Movement can be incredibly simple: a breath, a flutter of the hands, a shift of weight as we sit or stand. By playing with movement, we can explore shapes, rhythms, and patterns at a 3D level while mentally and emotionally connecting with the ideas that influence us.

In the pages ahead, I'm not going to be asking anything of you movement-wise that has to be performed in front of other people. This work is purely for your benefit and exploration. The only thing I ask is that you listen to your body as you try the exercises. I think you will be pleasantly surprised at the results!

All right, now that we've set some of those fears and misconceptions aside, let us continue on our journey!

Magic, Math, and the Tarot

If some of those misconceptions felt familiar, perhaps it's because we are also told by society that belief in magic is silly—that we are foolish to invest our time in rituals, spellcraft, divination, and folklore. Yet so much of what we know to be science today was first seen as magic.

The truth is that math and magic go hand in hand. What is math but a way of describing the rhythm of the universe? What is magic but a way to influence that rhythm? Both math and magic are ways to describe how we see, connect, and weave the patterns of ourselves, our actions, and even our thoughts and dreams with the world around us. The world moves and makes in numbers. By tapping into the power of those numbers energetically and creatively, we are able to more effectively divine the patterns happening in our lives.

The Tarot is rich in numbers. Obviously, numbers typically mark the order of the Major and Minor Arcana cards. But that's not all: We find numbers inherent in the shapes, symbols, and energetic motions that reveal the story being told in the cards. Shapes are rooted in geometry—built from numbers and patterns moving in space. Each shape has its own rhythm and tale to tell us. Symbols are devised from combined marks and shapes, building from their core meanings to contain even more mysteries and stories. These quintessential forms are a guide for connecting with the shapes our own bodies make as we move through and interact with the world.

Connecting math, magic, myth, and movement empowers us to see and interpret the Tarot more easily, especially across decks and systems. From the numbers present on the cards themselves to the number of cards we use in a spread, stories are being expressed. Arithmetic operations (addition, subtraction, multiplication, and division) can reveal relationships between the cards, describe patterns inherent in a spread, and help us plot what to do with the information we've been presented with. Finding the rhythm in the movement of numbers and related shapes in the cards helps to embody their meaning in our own muscles and bones. All this information creates a deeper core of understanding that enhances our powers of perception, observation, and prediction. The result of this mathematical cultivation is being a more accurate, considerate, and overall effective reader of the Tarot.

My own work has developed primarily from how I look at the energy of the numbers themselves and their relationship to shapes, utilizing mathematical processes to garner more information intuitively. My relationship with math and numbers comes directly from my lived experience and quirky neurospicy observations. I feel it's important to point out here that my method is not rooted in astrology, Qabalah, or New Age approaches to numerology or quantum physics—not that there's anything wrong with those things. They just aren't my personal fields of study or core influences. There may be some overlap of ideas and there may be some contradictions, but there are many ways to climb a mountain. This is simply the nature of the world, human development, and the phenomenon of multiple discovery. Multiple discovery theory states that most scientific discoveries, creative explorations, groundbreaking inventions, and dynamic ideas are generally conceived independently but are more or less generated simultaneously by multiple creative minds worldwide. For decades I've described this genius as a product of the "slutty muses." When the time is right, an idea appears—to a whole variety of minds—so we see repeated patterns across cultures utilized to solve similar problems time and time again. But even though there are similarities, each expression typically has its own unique flair, style, or signature. I trust that you, too, are going to add your own correlations and revelations to what you discover here. That's how it should be!

I often say to my students that Witchcraft is 80 to 90 percent observation and pattern recognition.[11] What I mean by that is I don't see the practice of Witchcraft, the ability to tap into magic, or having psychic abilities as something supernatural, unique, or extra special. Instead, I believe it's about honing our skills of paying attention to details and learning to recognize habits and cycles. When we observe the world more closely, we start to see similarities and notice beginnings and endings, and we can track outcomes to the point of reliably predicting them—strictly through observation and memory. When we immerse ourselves in the rhythm of life, we are able to work with the flow of the universe in order to cause change within ourselves and the world around us. That's not to say we're always going to be right or become all-knowing. However, to those who may not be paying attention, it definitely can seem like we Witches know exactly what's going on. Maybe we're born with it—or maybe it's just that we're good at probability and statistics.

Basically, the world is a numbers game. Sometimes it feels like you're playing bingo, sometimes it feels like blackjack, and sometimes you're standing in front of a guy with three cups asking you to pick the one the ball is hiding under. Maximizing your chances, engaging in strategy, and keeping an eye out for illusions are all good skills to have. This is especially true when it comes to utilizing your critical thinking skills and exercising your perceptive abilities, both of which are essential for doing math and magic—and reading the Tarot.

My approach to the Tarot is firmly rooted in my multiple years of experience as a reader, an artist, a Witch, and a dancer. Each of these areas has given me insight into where math and magic meet. As a reader, I recognize how the cards play out for a variety of people: the commonality of their issues and struggles and the possible solutions. The more you read for other people, the more you start to recognize common thought patterns, learn about behavioral responses, and discover the variety of different options folks can have or encounter. Of course not every situation is the

11. No one has ever asked me what the other 10 to 20 percent is. (Cookies, candles, cats, incense, and your beverage of choice. Oh, and shiny things.)

same, but there are often recognizable common threads. That collective experience can help you spot patterns when pulling cards, often resulting in better advice and direction.

As an artist, I see sacred geometry and patterns present all around me. I see math in sigils—and I'm not just talking about the sigils generated from numbered squares or wheels. My Sigil Witchery method is very heavily invested in the idea that marks have meaning. This includes everything from simple lines all the way to more complex shapes and icons. Every shape has a kind of motion to it. The number of times an element is used, the numbers that resonate through certain shapes—all these are tapping into the key to solve whatever problem the sigil was designed for. Art also unlocks parts of our unconscious minds and enables us to express our thoughts and desires where words or other means may not. I think one of the major reasons my Sigil Witchery method can be so effective for folks is that it teaches us to recognize the numbers, shapes, and rhythms of the universe and uses art to tap into them for more precise results. Similarly, when we look closely at the art in a Tarot deck, we can find those symbols, patterns, and other clues that help us delve deeper into our unconscious selves and the paths before us.

As a Witch, I know that math tends to subtly affect and influence how we view and work magic. Every Witch I know has a favorite number, from personal lucky numbers that have meaning when they appear to a preferred number of breaths that are done when performing ritual, spellcraft, or meditation. Many Witches and other magical practitioners have a preference for how large a circle should be cast, how many elements are invoked, how many directions are recognized, how many times a chant is uttered, or how many times a space should be walked or traced before something is established or banished. The numbers 3, 5, 7, 9, and 13 especially show up a lot. I personally have several systems that each involve 5 parts.[12] We are also constantly using certain shapes to define magic, from

12. Two examples: My RITES approach found in my book *Weave the Liminal* is made up of Roots, Inspiration, Time, Environment, and Star. *Anatomy of a Witch* features the Witch's Heart, Lungs, Serpent, Bones, and Mind.

stars with 5, 6, 7, 8, and 9 points to squares, circles, triangles, spirals, and so forth. Time and time again, we are referencing systems that intertwine math and magic—and the Tarot is definitely one of those systems!

Speaking of time, as a dancer, that's another way I've recognized the relationship between math and magic. The art of timing is crucial to dance. We will talk specifically about rhythm and time signatures in more depth later in this chapter, so what I mean by timing here is presentation and connection. The length of time that a dance is presented, how fast or slow you execute a movement, whether you're on the beat or against it, and when you take a breath, begin, or end—all this is a matter of timing. Is holding that pose for three seconds too long or not enough time? Does the choreography drag on because it's too repetitive? Is there a feeling of suspense, or is the audience overwhelmed by too much happening all at once? All these details help describe the intersection of art and math—and determine whether the dance holds attention or loses it. That is a type of magic as well that enhances and informs the experience of the dancer and those observing. Timing can play a similar role in the Tarot—how long we're looking at, when to act, when to hang back, when to keep repeating something or totally change course.

These are just a few insights into how different aspects of my existence have informed my views on math, magic, and the Tarot. You very likely have some connections of your own right now. If you're into astrology, you know that charts are calculated using birth times, location coordinates, and the movements of heavenly bodies—with each section of a chart relating to numbered houses. Astrological math can give insight to those who decipher its meanings. If you're a baker, you know that precision is key because chemistry is involved. Having the right ratio of ingredients, the exact temperature, and precise timing all make the magic happen. If you understand how each aspect is influential, then you know how to adjust things just so to get the perfect result. From accounting to songwriting, programming to ceramics, math pairs with our intuition, experience, and creativity to achieve the desired results.

So naturally, when it comes to the Tarot, it makes sense to see the magic of the math—or the math of the magic. Now let's look deeper at how forms can play a role in deciphering meaning.

The Shape of Meaning

The world moves and makes in numbers. Math is in motion all around us, and the Tarot is a fantastic example of seeing the movement of math on multiple levels all at once. I think that's why the Tarot is such an incredible and insightful tool into ourselves and the universe.

The Tarot is essentially a collection of two-dimensional (2D) images that we can hold in our hands. Those images are derived from three-dimensional (3D) scenes, objects, and motifs that are transferred to 2D using skilled observation via drawing, painting, and other visual art techniques. As we read the cards, the still images are transformed to apply to the world around us—back into 3D! The art of Tarot is simultaneously compressing and expanding the world through images and our thoughts.

Shapes and Symbols

Next, there are symbols, which the Tarot is rich in. Symbols are essentially refined, simplified expressions of complex ideas—made up of basic shapes and lines. Shapes and marks have meaning and energy to them that correspond to numbers. An oval can correspond to 0, a single vertical line can be seen as 1, and a pair of parallel lines can symbolize 2. A triangle is made up of 3 lines, and squares and rectangles are quadrilateral shapes, meaning they are based on 4. As we explore the Major and Minor Arcana in the chapters ahead, I encourage you to think back to this connection between shape and number and the related meanings of the cards.

Many symbols and shapes are repeated throughout the RWS Tarot, often connecting cards and themes together. It's fun to spot them. Keep in mind that while there may be traditional meanings associated with a symbol, it can also have another layer of meaning that is personal to you or relevant to the querent.

Here's what I typically think of when I see these symbols:

Symbol		Meaning
Moon		lunar mysteries, dreams, the subconscious
Sun		solar mysteries, vibrancy, revelation
Lemniscate		infinity, unity, vitality
Flowers		growth, accolades, beauty
Snake		transformation, intuition, secrets
Pomegranate		underworld mysteries, promise, potential
Scroll		doctrine, wisdom, guide
Key		unlocking mysteries, power
Mountains		navigating difficulty, challenges, goals
Water		emotions, the past, below the surface
Lantern		illumination, seeking, preparation
Scales		justice, decisions, balance
Pillars		support, structure, passageways
Feather		achievement, ideals, creativity
Laurel		honor, recognition, respect

Some Commonly Found Symbols in the Tarot

Besides the numbers and their corresponding shapes (which we will explore a little more hands-on shortly), there are likely going to be more complex symbols appearing in your deck. Symbols are used intentionally to convey hidden wisdom and ideas, some of which we may be privy to and others that we're meant to guess or find our own meaning for. For example, in the RWS Tarot you'll find pomegranates, roses, lilies, grapevines, and sunflowers throughout the deck. These are more than just decorative elements that Pamela Colman Smith thought would be pretty; these herbs and plants have layers of symbolism. If you are familiar with the Hermetic Order of the Golden Dawn, you may pull upon the symbolism it assigns to the plants, animals, and other symbols found within the art. But if you are a gardener or an herbalist, you may also have your own personal associations with these symbols. I believe your personal experience and interpretations are equally valid—and may even lend deeper meaning for the card's interpretation.

Not only are there hidden symbols that can be tucked away in each card, but there are also the big obvious ones front and center! Every suit has its core symbol: the sword, the wand, the cup, and the pentacle traditionally. These icons represent the personality and power of each suit. Again, you may connect them to the Golden Dawn's associations, or, if you're a Witch, you likely have your own connections to these tools that influence your experience of them. When an artist changes up the suit symbols entirely to fit their inspiration, you might find yourself connecting back to the symbols you're familiar with—or developing a whole new relationship with what's in front of you. Whenever you get a new deck, take some time to look over what's been chosen to represent each suit. Write down your impressions of what those symbols mean to you and what you think they mean. This exercise will help you create connection to the cards and may expand your symbol knowledge.

Colors

There is also symbolism that can accompany the use of color. We respond to colors emotionally and mentally, even if we're not always immediately conscious of their effect. But it's also important to note that the symbolism of colors can be highly subjective or culturally rooted. For example, the use of red might indicate love, fire, vitality, power, or fortune. The following is a chart of colors and their possible meanings, but keep in mind that this is just a sampling!

Red	Power, love, life force, leadership, fortune, fire
Orange	Growth, balance, friendship, devotion, warmth
Yellow	Solar, light, positivity, intelligence, growth, air
Green	Joy, fertility, earth, money, prosperity, hope
Blue	Water, wisdom, emotions, calm, purification, fluidity
Purple	Loyalty, justice, royalty, wealth, bravery
Black	Mystery, death, darkness, loss, grief, change
White	Light, purity, innocence, new beginnings, divinity

Many well-designed decks often select specific color palettes for each suit. As you go through your deck, look to see if one color or family of colors stands out across all the cards in a suit. What do you think these color choices say about the cards?

While many decks are in full color, there are some decks in black and white, gray scale, or a very limited color palette. Historical decks tend to be simpler in color design because they utilized lithography or block plates for printing, whereas today's CMYK printing methods can generate a wider spectrum of colors. So sometimes there's a technical reason why a deck looks the way it does—the printing process often limited the color palette. If a new deck is very limited in colors, it's often an intentional design choice to create a specific mood or aesthetic.

Composition in the Cards

In design terms, the *composition* of a piece of artwork refers to the arrangement and organization of visual elements within the defined image area. Every Tarot card has its own composition—what we can see in the frame of the card. How color, shape, and form are used in the composition can carry additional meaning. There are eight principles of composition that artists, designers, and photographers use to tell a story through image: balance, proportion, emphasis, rhythm, movement, unity, contrast, and pattern.

Balance can be symmetrical, which gives a feeling of order and stability, or asymmetrical, which depicts movement and energy. Does the card seem stable and static, or is there action happening? The Emperor is a very symmetrical card, while the Fool is asymmetrical.

Proportion refers to the scale of subjects in the frame and their apparent special relationship to each other in space. If something is bigger or more important, it tends to be closer to us, while smaller items appear to be in the distance. For example, the 2 of Wands shows a figure very close to us, gazing off into the distance. We can tell there's distance because the landscape details are very simple and small.

Emphasis refers to the focal point of the composition. What is your eye immediately drawn to? Why is this element important? Consider the Tower card and how our eyes are drawn first to the top, where the lightning is striking the tower. Then we visually travel down the lines of the tower, noticing the falling figures.

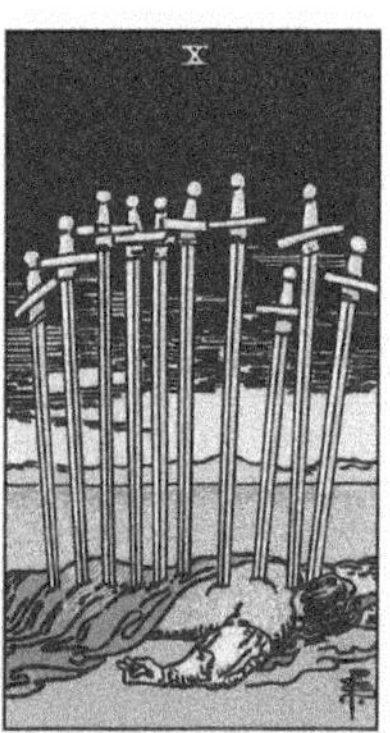

Rhythm in composition refers to the repeated elements in the frame that help move your eye around the focal point. What components show up multiple times and what does their placement say to you? The most obvious element of the 10 of Swords is the ten swords driven into the body on the ground. Would this card have the same impact if the swords were just scattered or lying on the ground?

Movement is the energy generated by lines, shapes, and colors that create a sense of motion. What shapes do you notice? The 6 of Swords has a lot of diagonal lines that emphasize the movement of the boat. The 5 of Wands utilizes intersecting diagonal lines to depict conflict and chaos.

Unity brings cohesion and harmony through the use of similar shapes, colors, and symbols. Everything feels related and at home. The Star card has a largely harmonious color palette of blues and greens and repeated elements of water and stars throughout the image.

Contrast uses opposites to tell its dramatic story, playing with light and shadow, hard and soft elements, and varying textures. The Devil card depicts a scene similar to that in the Lovers card, but there's a heavy use of black to define the figures and the scale of the Devil is much greater than the couple.

Patterns utilize repetition with rhythm and movement, but in the Tarot, repeated elements also emphasize certain concepts. If we see a motif appearing again and again, there's a symbolic relationship between these cards. Notice the use of pomegranates in the veil behind the High Priestess, the dress of the Empress, and Death's flag. Pomegranates traditionally symbolize wisdom, abundance, and the cycle of life and death.

———— • ● • ————

When we start to notice these compositional details, we realize there are a lot more clues to discover in each card. You can look at the same Tarot card dozens of times and then one day notice something totally new! It's like the card is sharing a new revelation with you that is significant to that reading.

Meaning in Movement

Now that we've covered the visual design components of the cards, let's explore the symbolism a little more physically. Earlier in the chapter we briefly covered basic shapes and I mentioned that they can relate to numbers.

Well, how do we glean meaning from basic shapes? We started by making them with our bodies. Every shape has a feeling or energy to it, and the best way to understand what that's like is to make the shape. Your body can form, make, or draw these simple shapes, depending on your flexibility, ability, and creativity. You don't have to engage your whole body either to feel what I mean. There are numerous ways to move your body to interpret shapes, from simply tracing a shape with your fingertip, your toe, or a pen to gesturing with both arms and fully engaging the entire body.

One of my mentors, Artemis E. Mourat,[13] often describes dance as creating shapes and patterns in space, and I wholeheartedly believe that. In fact, I think this idea applies to everything in the universe, from the smallest particle to the largest galaxy—it's all in motion, moving through space and time. In your body, there are atoms that are moving at their own rate and interacting with each other to create the base particles that make up our cells. Our cells have their own internal and external movement that makes up our organs. Our organs have a beat, pulse, or rhythm that sets us in motion. We as human beings are moving through our environments at our own pace, all on a planet that is turning on its axis while also orbiting the sun. Our solar system—made up of all the other planets and the sun itself—is also in motion, creating sacred geometry in its path. And our galaxy is moving through space, dancing with other galaxies. The entire universe is dancing and everything is in motion on some level. With that perspective in mind, we see that everything makes a shape or a pattern in its own way, and there is also some number that expresses that shape or motion. With that connection in mind, we can find meaning through movement.

Let's look at a few examples of some simple shapes we can make and how they can be energetically felt.

13. Learn more at https://www.artemismourat.com.

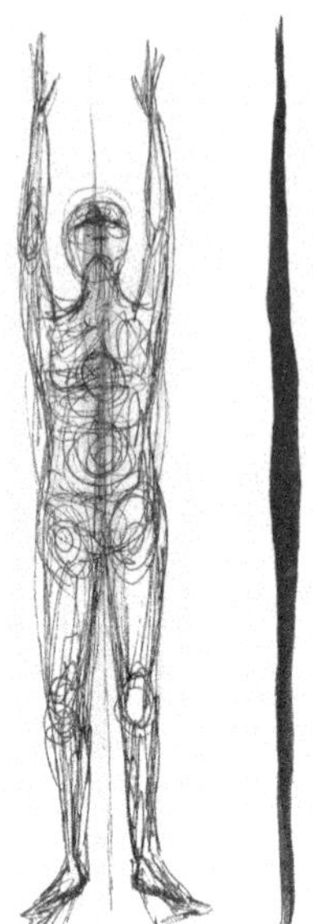

Vertical Line: A vertical line connects north and south. It is essentially the essence of a pole, a tree, or a tower, breaking with the horizon to rise up. To feel a vertical line, stand with your feet fairly close together (just within the frame of your shoulders is fine).[14] Extend both arms straight up, with your palms parallel to each other, fingertips pointing to the sky. Let your chin naturally rise up as well. Be aware of your feet making contact with the earth and let the consciousness of your body follow up your spine to your head and arms. Feel the pull from feet to fingertips. You are the vertical line. It should feel strong and energized yet sturdy and almost solemn.

14. You can also do this exercise from a seated position, using your pelvis or tailbone as a base instead of your feet.

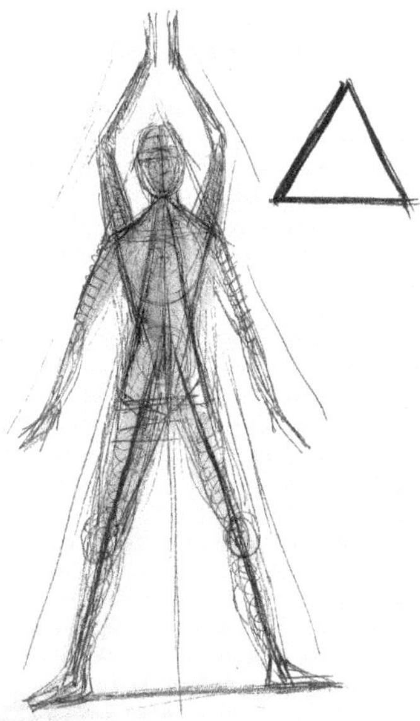

Triangle: The triangle rises out of the horizon somewhat like the vertical line, but the sensation is completely different. Part of this comes from the fact that no matter which kind of triangle you're making, two diagonal lines are involved with a horizontal or vertical line. The diagonal lines drive the energy up or down or left or right, depending on which way the shape is pointing. There is a relationship of three intersections happening (hence "tri" and "angle"), and rather than extending forever like the vertical line, the triangle is a closed shape. Energy travels either *within* the shape or *around* the shape. To feel a triangle through your whole body, stand with your feet wide apart (beyond your shoulders). One option is to let your arms align with the angle of your sides so that your fingertips follow your legs and point down to your feet. Your head becomes the top of the triangle. Or you can try moving your arms outstretched above your head and meeting in "prayer" hands (palms together). Your hands are the top of the pyramid. Consider how these two positions feel energetically to you. There should be a strong sensation of stability and taking up space. Hands pointing down will feel more rooted, while hands pointing out directs energy to the sky.

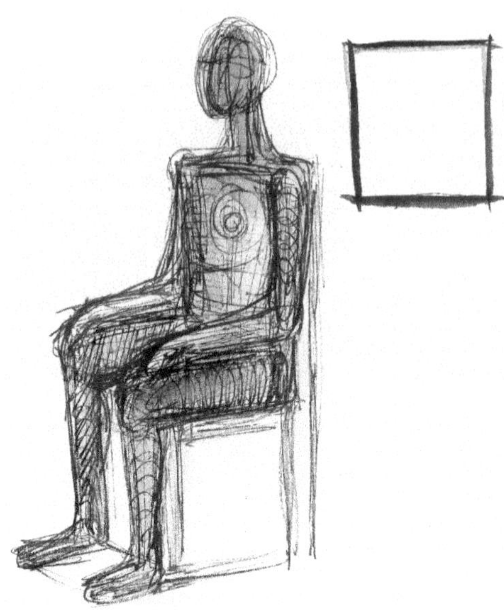

Square: A square is formed by two intersecting pairs of parallel lines, one vertical set and one horizontal set. You've experienced how strong a single vertical line feels. You also know how solid a horizontal line is (especially when you must get up and out of bed). When we set each line up in pairs and run them together, a block is formed. Squares are incredibly sturdy, secure shapes with their neat and tidy 90-degree angles. They don't like to roll or move around but prefer to sit and hold space. So a good way to feel a square is to sit down with your feet and shoulders equally spaced apart so they visually line up. Sit tall, with your hands resting on top of your legs, or you can raise your arms up, elbows bent, so that your hands are at eye level on either side of your face. You should feel strong, protected, and even powerful in this position.

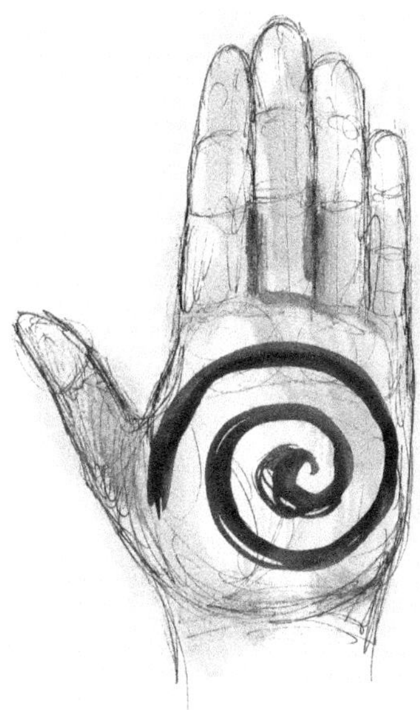

Spiral: The spiral is found in the Fibonacci sequence and is present in the whorls of snail shells as well as galaxies. The movement of a spiral can start at its tail and move toward the center, narrowing its focus. Or it can start at the center and flow out, ever expanding into the universe. One of the easiest and most accessible ways to feel a spiral is to take your non-dominant hand and hold it palm up. Then, using the tip of the index finger of your dominant hand, start at the base of your thumb and trace a spiral from the outside toward the center. Next, from the center, reverse direction and trace the spiral back out. Try this exercise going both clockwise and counterclockwise around your palm. If you need a bigger surface to get the feel of the spiral, try drawing it on a surface such as a tabletop or on the ground—or in the air in front of you. Feel how focused the spiral that moves to the center is energetically, and how open the expanding spiral feels in contrast.

Right now you might be thinking, "This all sounds interesting, but are you really expecting me to dance the Tarot in order to read it? Like, am I going to have to do a dance every time I pull out the cards?" No, I don't expect you to create a mini choreography every time you read the Tarot.[15] But I hope you play with the movements as you study the Tarot. When we engage more fully with our bodies, we can gather more insight and understanding about ourselves in so many ways. Feelings, memories, and other forms of connection can be unlocked by even the simplest of movements. We tend to believe that our brain is the only "thinking" part of our body, but the brain is just mission control—one character in a whole interactive play. All our organs transmit information. We perceive with so much more than just our eyes and ears, which is good since sometimes those senses lie to us as well!

Processing the shapes and patterns present in the world around us through our bodies can reveal so much. When teaching sacred dance, I like to show some examples of how certain kinds of deities have been depicted in paintings and sculptures around the world and then copy those postures. There's a reason we see those shapes and positions again and again across cultures and media: Power is contained within the body and how it moves. So when it comes to the Tarot, mimicking how a figure in a card is depicted—whether they are sitting, standing, or moving—can reveal more about the card. Movement is another way to learn more about ourselves and the patterns of the universe.

A Note About Abilities and Bodies: With movement exercises, please understand that they can be adapted to fit your body's ability and range of mobility. If I say "stand," you can modify that direction for sitting. You can move your fingers or hands instead of your whole arm; the same with toes/feet versus legs. Do what is physically possible and comfortable for you without causing strain, discomfort, or injury.

15. Though if you do this and film it, please tag me!

Commonly Seen Poses of Deities and Spirits from Around the World and Related Shapes

You don't have to do any of these movements in front of anyone either—that's not the point. The purpose of this exercise is playing with movement to see how it makes you feel, think, and change your perspective. Consider how different shapes and positions influence your mind and your emotions. Besides, your cat is going to judge you regardless of what you do, so best to give it a try! Be adventurous and be present in your body.

Figure This

Bodies don't necessarily always have to be dancing in order for there to be a connection to meaning and symbolism. After all, the Tarot shows us snapshot moments that are meant to stimulate us visually.

Another name for math and numbers is figures—and I love that figures can also mean bodies! Stuart R. Kaplan writes in his book *The Artwork & Times of Pamela Colman Smith* that "her writings indicate that, for her, ritual and symbolism derived their power to illuminate from the senses, emotion and the imagination, not from the mind."[16] I feel this when I look at how Smith placed the figures in her cards—and that, too, can give us another way of seeing the energy and meaning of the cards.

As we explore the Major and Minor Arcana in the next three chapters, examine the positions, poses, and movement of the figures in your cards. What does the body language and composition say to you?

Left, Center, or Right? The first way to find meaning in the figures is to consider which way they are facing in the card, from our point of view. If a figure is looking to the left, they are considering the past. If the figure faces us straight on directly, they are focused on the present. If a figure is facing the right, they are future-minded. As for facing completely away from us (not looking left or right) when not in a crowd interacting with other figures, this happens in only a few cards in the Minor Arcana—and these cards center on someone considering a choice. So this perspective can emphasize that *we* are that figure contemplating our options.

16. Kaplan, *The Artwork & Times of Pamela Colman Smith*, 76.

Seated, Standing, or in Motion? Once we have determined which way the figure is facing, the next step is to interpret how they are moving—or how secure or grounded they seem in this snapshot. Are they slumped, slouching, or sitting tall? Are they holding their ground with both feet firmly planted or are they subtly shifting their weight? Are they dancing, walking, or leaping? Each posture has an energy to it. To understand the posture from an emotional and creative perspective, try to mimic the position with your own body. How does it make you feel? Do you feel strong or vulnerable? Balanced or dynamic? Even being perfectly still has a feeling to it that you can sense if you take a moment to experience it.

This approach of examining the figures may not be applicable to all Tarot decks, as I don't believe it's something that all Tarot artists think about. But if a deck is directly inspired by the RWS, there's a good chance you'll see the pattern repeated in the bodies, even if it's not 100 percent faithful to the original. Since the Tarot is constantly evolving, there's always an opportunity for someone to build on those ideas and amplify them in new ways.

Hear the Rhythm of the Universe

If we're going to explore movement, then we should also consider what the accompanying soundtrack may be. Math and music are interwoven as well, so let's use that as an opportunity to consider rhythm, pattern, and energy—and how we can utilize them for divination.

As a dancer, it's my job to feel the structure of the music and translate it through my body. I listen for the core rhythm and any melodies that are played on top of the rhythm's beat, as well as the emotional expression of any words that are sung. If you break it down into notes, scales, and patterns, you're essentially looking at numbers in sound format. But you don't have to know the exact numbers consciously to understand the music and be able to move to it. When you listen with the whole of your body, you become a part of the music. You are the song.

Even if you've never heard a particular song before, you can settle into it and very likely predict what will come next. Being able to do an improvised dance to a song I've never heard before isn't a superpower; I'm simply using my observation skills that I've developed with practice. I'm also allowing myself to be in the moment rather than trying to consciously think too far ahead. There's a similar balance when it comes to divination: Experience and practice are key, but you want to be present in the moment and learn not to over-anticipate, or else you'll miss the beat.

Recognizing the energy and movement present in the Tarot's numbers helps with both connecting to the universe's rhythm and being present in a reading without overthinking it. I'd even go so far as to say that the Tarot is a dance and cards can certainly have their own moves and time signatures. The number of a card becomes an insightful clue to what we're feeling and possibly how to work our way through an issue.

What do I mean that the cards can have a rhythm? You've likely heard a dancer count off (either in person, in a movie, or on TV) "5, 6, 7, 8!" Much of western music is set in 4/4 time, with related recreational dance forms being set in counts of 8. This means it takes 8 beats to go through a set of steps. In many world music dance rhythms, the count is different and the energy of the music changes from a standard 4/4.

Every time signature and the speed at which it is played creates a mood. The Egyptian Ayyub rhythm is a 2/4 and is often used in Zar trance dances. This slow-building rhythm appeases spirits while also being an outlet for emotional or mental frustrations and could be aligned with the High Priestess. A typical waltz is a 3/4 time signature, which fits in nicely for a lilting dance with the Empress. Your typical rock 'n' roll song tends to have a 4/4 time signature with a strong backbeat, steady and reliable—just like the Emperor. Moroccan and Algerian Chaabi music use 6/8 rhythms, which are upbeat and groovy and feel like they can sustain you for hours to keep the motion going. They easily connect with the Lovers card.

Another interesting thing about rhythm is that it can be sped up and slowed down. The 9/8 Turkish rhythm can be extremely uplifting and bouncy when played fast. It has a surprising little hang to it that you don't want to miss. When played very slowly, it has a trancey drag to it. Both require you to relax into your core in order to catch the pause—very Hermit in nature!

You could even see the Minor Arcana cards as different kinds of music in how you might move to it as you become familiar with each of them. Every suit could be a whole genre! The Cups could be power ballads or love songs, the Wands rap, the Swords metal, and the Pentacles club music. A playful and stimulating idea is to create a playlist of songs that represent the Tarot—for you. At the 2020 PantheaCon in San Jose, California, Madame Pamita and James Divine threw an event called "Studio78 Tarot Disco Dance Party." It was a really fun way to dance through cards and see how people related each song to a card. You could also make a playlist for each Major Arcana card as you explore them, especially if multiple songs remind you of one card—or just select one song per card. You really can dance your way through the Tarot!

———— • • • ————

Now it is time to meet the Major Arcana! Keep in mind that a lot of what we covered in this chapter will make more sense as you explore each of the cards and build a relationship with your deck, especially if Tarot is new to you. I invite you to read through this chapter again later. You'll be surprised at what you notice with a repeat review!

CHAPTER 3

The Major Arcana—from 0 to 10

Welcome to the Major Arcana—the big mysteries await your exploration! In the following pages you will discover the meaning of the numbers, the movement present within each card, and the magic to guide us. All these elements are keys to unlocking the meaning of each card and how it relates to other cards.

The first eleven cards of the Major Arcana can be a way to view ourselves as we develop throughout life: embodied spirits experiencing being human physically, emotionally, and mentally. It has been referred to as the Fool's Journey, but I caution you not to consider the trek as a one-time-through or a road that runs only in a linear fashion. The universe is prone to spirals, so we are often tracing the same path again and again, working our way to the center and back out again. The wisdom we learn is cumulative, but we often need a refresher of certain lessons time and time again. I think it's best to remember that the goal of this journey isn't to get to the end, but rather to be present in each experience along the way.

I will make note of key elements depicted in the RWS deck that are often repeated in decks inspired by it, but I will not describe every card to you in great detail. There is extensive symbolism that can be found in every one of the RWS cards, but not every detail will be found in every card across all decks. So as we're focusing on learning this approach by understanding the numbers, I will not bog you down by pointing out every detail and will instead stick to our mathematical inspirations and magical purposes. I enthusiastically encourage you to study the deck(s) you have chosen to work with and glean meaning from the details that may be present in the cards. Look at each card as we go through them. What do *you* notice? What is the card saying to you in this moment?

This is the format we will explore for each card in this chapter:

The Card: Title of the card

The Number: Number assigned to the card

The Shape: The mark, shape, or symbol that best represents this card

Snapshot: A quick description of the image at a glance

Musing: A little poetic exploration of the card that touches on the personality of the card, appropriate for meditation

Core Principles: Key words or ideas I associate with the number and card (See a condensed list of all the cards with their top ideas in the "Quick Number Reference" in the back of the book.)

Add It Up: Considerations of the math that makes up the card in terms of mathematical processes such as addition, subtraction, multiplication, and division

Exploring the Magic: How the number, shape, and image can give us meaning and guidance while also delving into the philosophy, ideas, and metaphysics

Put It in Motion: An exercise on how to connect with the card

The Fool

The Number: 0

The Shape: Ellipse, ouroboros

Snapshot: A carefree and jubilant figure carries a bindle over their shoulder as they walk close to a precipice. A small dog dances alongside their feet.

Musing: *Begin again. Become a beginner again.*

Core Principles: Beginning, the egg, entry or starting point, a clean slate, endless possibilities

Add It Up: Our first card of the Major Arcana curiously starts at 0 instead of 1. Mathematically we are at no quantity, with nothing yet to measure. Once we move past 0, we can begin to add or subtract, but right now in this moment we are at a neutral place. This is also not a time for trying to speed things up just to get past this point. Rushing will likely only find us back again at 0. Remember that any number multiplied by 0 is still 0. Zero also holds the place for what's to come in the decimal system (10s, 100s, 1000s, etc.), once again emphasizing the potential for growth.

Exploring the Magic: The Fool is a spirit that has become newly embodied, touching down upon the earth for the first time. As the Fool, we are the seeker, the newcomer, the beginner, the explorer with a fresh and open mind. All these aspects are also alternative names for this card.

At birth (or shortly after, depending on cultural beliefs), we shift from a noncorporeal existence to an incarnate one and become largely bound by the laws of this reality. As beings of both flesh and spirit, we find that the world is a place of infinite possibilities. It is ours to touch, taste, smell, hear, see, and explore. Our potential seems limitless—especially if we can break the binds of societal expectations and restrictions placed upon us by ourselves or others.

Our next step leads us off a precipice into a new existence ruled by matter. As a Witch, I don't believe we enter this world without choice or forethought. I think we may have a sense of where we could go, but there's still a sense of adventure and discovery. It's not a cliff we are stepping off, but rather the next step down this mountain called life.

Zero is a fresh start, a new beginning, ripe with infinite potential and all the endless possibilities of life. Zero is an egg representing hope and the continuing cycle of life. We are faced with news and can revel in wonder as the egg begins to crack and brings forth the newly hatched self. What adventure awaits us we don't know yet—and that is part of the excitement!

The ellipse of the zero holds not only the potential of a great cosmic egg but also the serpent energy often associated with the ouroboros. The ouroboros is a symbol that depicts a serpent or dragon eating its own tail and represents the endless cycle of renewal through death and life. This ancient symbol reminds us that every end is a beginning. We have been here before and we shall be the Fool again.

Another thing to note is that the Fool does not enter this world empty-handed. The Fool carries a bindle (a knapsack on a pole), which I believe contains the tools of the Minor Arcana. Even though we are becoming beginners again, the bindle hints that we do not enter this world unprepared. Other tools that may have been packed could be aspects of our past lives, a map of genetic memory, and the wisdom of our ancestors and the land. We might not be sure of where we are going or what we are doing next, but there's a good chance we've got some snacks. So soak up the wonder, be curious, and embrace the possibilities with a beginner's mind.

Put It in Motion: One of the most important aspects of the Fool card is the moment of "touch down"—a spirit becoming one with their physical form. You can certainly draw a zero in the air before you (Dr. Strange–style) with your hand or whole arm to get a feel for the ellipse. However, I prefer something a little more physically grounding in nature for connecting to this card: picking up and putting down my feet one at a time, from the toe to the ball to the heel. As I ease my weight from side to side, I am engaging in balance and feeling the tactile sensation of my feet touching the earth. As I kiss the earth with my feet, I not only connect with the earth but also feel the lightness of the next possible step.

The Magician

The Number: 1

The Shape: Vertical line

Snapshot: A figure in ritual attire stands behind an altar, one arm extended up toward the sky and the other pointing to the ground. The symbols of the Minor Arcana (wand, sword, cup, and pentacle) are placed on the altar before them.

Musing: *Assembled and present at the altar.*

Core Principles: Gaining experience, connection of above and below, singular focus, intellectual development

Add It Up: As we know from the Fool's existence, the Magician is not the first card of the Major Arcana in modern decks.[17] The Magician does not appear out of nowhere, fully formed and wise to everything—even though they may want you to believe that! The chant "We're number

17. Some earlier versions of the Tarot place the Fool at the end after the World or as an outlier, like the Joker in playing cards.

one!" is meant to imply that "we" are first and best at something. Number 1 is not a ranking or quality placement here, but it could be where we begin to keep score or at least keep track of what we've learned. The presence of 1 is evidence that the self or something exists, and this point is just the first step in learning to truly understand what that means. One is "I exist, I am present, I am ready to learn more."

Exploring the Magic: Moving to 1 with the Magician, we find that the Fool spirit has fully taken the leap into the physical world, is now firmly ensconced in a body, and is starting to figure out how the world works. Just a quick look at the position and posture of the Magician affirms this reality. The Magician is facing forward, which symbolizes being oriented in and focused on the present. One arm points to above and the other gestures below, connecting ethereal planes with physical ones. This unification is echoed in the flowers that frame the Magician at the top of the image and along the bottom. We can interpret this repetition as the idea that what we do in the physical world affects the spiritual world at a macrocosmic level, but it would behoove us to consider that the physical activities we engage in also affect us emotionally and mentally within our own microcosms.

The Magician also stands behind an altar—a place of sacred action and connection—ready to begin a rite or ritual of some sort. The altar marks our current physical realm, where above and below meet. The tools the Fool carried in their bindle are now displayed on the altar, waiting to be explored and understood. Building familiarity with these tools and lessons brings the essence of individuality and the opportunities to create and manifest as we continue our journey. The mindset of building skill and wisdom is why the Magician can also be referred to as the Magus, the Juggler, the Adept, or the Builder.

In the RWS, starting with the Magician, the card numbers are represented by Roman numerals instead of Arabic ones. Unlike Arabic numerals, Roman numerals do not allow for the concept of zero, so it's an interesting choice to switch. Since "1" is "I" in Roman numerals, there is potentially more symbolism to consider. When we use "I," there is a sense of self and identity built into this simple letter. "I" is awareness of being, the development of ego, and having both singular and relative focus: "I know who I am and I am figuring out my purpose in this world."

Put It in Motion: In chapter 2 I invited you to feel the sensation of being a vertical line. To tap into the energy of the Magician, we're going to build off this earlier instruction. Stand with your feet squared with your shoulders, head facing forward, chin parallel to the floor. Raise and extend your left arm and point to the sky while your right arm points to the earth. Be present for a moment feeling this position. Take a breath and begin to switch your arms so that the right now points up and the left points down. Exhale as your arms reach the middle point of the switch before arriving at the opposite placement. Repeat the breath-and-switch motion at least twice more until you get a good sense of the movement.

The High Priestess

The Number: 2

The Shape: Parallel vertical lines, Gemini symbol

Snapshot: A robed figure adorned with lunar imagery sits between two pillars, one black and one white. A curtain with a pomegranate pattern hangs between the columns.

Musing: *Enter into the mystery.*

Core Principles: Dualities, facing the unknown, mysteries, balance, discovering meaning, communication, going deeper, overcoming fears, a doorway to the liminal

Add It Up: The math starts to get really interesting from here on out as the numbers go up in value. When there are two of something, there are more conversations to be had, more information to be gathered. Two represents the potential to increase and multiply in ways that are not possible with just one. Two can represent a pair that are identical, but it can also represent a contrast, things that are similar yet different—like the two pillars. They both have the same shape and function, but their surfaces are not the same in appearance. It's also wise to consider not only what each part of the pair represents or has to say but also what happens in the space between them. What is not being said or made obvious?

An equal sign is two horizontal lines that are the same length, but because they are parallel, they do not meet. They create a suggested third space in between them: a place to connect that is neither one line nor the other.

A crossroads (in the shape of a literal cross) is made up of two lines intersecting perpendicularly. They meet, but they start in different places and continue along their own way afterward. We must ask: What is the nature of the pairing when they meet? What happens before and after?

So whenever we have two lines present—be they vertical, horizontal, parallel, or perpendicular—we find a meeting of ideas. An interesting way to think of the High Priestess's connection with 2 is that since the Magician is 1, what happens when you have *two* Magicians? Think about what they might say to each other or otherwise behave. Would they each continue to go about doing their own thing, would they meet up and compare notes and collaborate, or would they be at odds with each other?

Exploring the Magic: Within the realm of the Priestess is the mystery of things hidden in the depths of consciousness, the subtle influences of the world around us as well as inner illumination. As it's associated with the number 2, this card represents dualities and communication. In order to communicate, there must be a speaker and a listener—even if they are one and the same within us.

When you gaze upon the Priestess, you may note the lunar phases in her crown, the solar cross on her chest, and the crescent at her feet, and she is flanked by black and white temple pillars. Within these symbols you can find balance of light and shadow, night and day—touching upon the lunar and solar cycles of ritual. Lightness and darkness are dualities, each with their own story to tell, yet they help to define each other. One cannot exist in concept without the other.

The Magician has prepared the way for the Priestess by setting up the altar, positioning the tools, and preparing the space to be worked in. Now is the time to figure out how things work, what these tools mean to you, and how to implement them effectively. Part of this process sometimes involves learning things the hard way—as in what not to do in comparison to what works best. In order to figure out this practice, you have to do more than just stand there. You might need to have a plan, which means you will need to gather information to plot accordingly. You must be willing to take chances, try new things, and explore other points of view. Understand that failure is simply part of the process and not a detriment to achievement or evidence of character flaws. The Priestess challenges us to build expertise through experimentation and experience. Moving forward can be scary, but all you need to do is take a breath and jump in.

The Priestess beckons you to enter the mystery and find the temple within: to not just look the part, but to walk the path, even if you're unsure of where it leads. Not everything can be neatly planned or predicted, despite our best intentions. You have to turn your eyes away from the map to see where you are going. Cross the threshold, part the curtain, and pass through to the next challenge. Just remember to look both ways before crossing the street.

Put It in Motion: To explore duality is to consider balance and symmetry. Stand tall and straight, with your arms at your sides and your weight evenly distributed on both legs. Keeping your arms straight and parallel, slowly raise them up to the sky while taking a deep breath in. You are essentially "drawing" the two pillars on either side of you. Then lower your arms slowly and exhale. Next, turn around (180 degrees) to face behind you and repeat the same motions. You can also modify this exercise for a seated position, swiveling on your stool or chair to smoothly change direction.

The Empress

The Number: 3

The Shape: Triangle

Snapshot: A crowned, voluptuous figure sits upon a cushioned throne, surrounded by crops and lush forest.

Musing: *Be abundant and complete within yourself.*

Core Principles: Creativity, abundance, fertility, sovereignty of self, emotional support, nurturing, understanding your power and the ability to make choices that build into larger things

Add It Up: In the previous card, I asked you to consider what happens when two Magicians meet. At 3, we have both the Magician and the High Priestess meeting to lead us to the Empress. Essentially this looks like the following equation:[18]

18. Seeing how the numbers can add up or multiply to get to a particular card helps us glean even more meaning from the card, so you will see more examples of these equations moving forward as I share some combinations for your consideration.

Magician: Building Skills & Experience (1) + High Priestess: Communication & Exploring Mystery (2) = Empress: Creativity & Choices (3)

This equation suggests that when we combine our skills and learned experience with expression and exploration, we are fertile grounds for creativity and a variety of choices that we can build upon.

Three also builds us a triangle—a tableau to fill with ideas, a flag to raise up. We have a base and a convergence that can point us in the direction we need to go next. But which way is it pointing? That's the thing about the number 3—we are confronted with choices that require consideration. With 2's dual nature, the selection was a 50-50 choice. You could choose either this or that. But with 3, it's no longer a coin flip. You need to do a bit more work to sort out which choice is the best one, if you wish to make an educated selection.

Exploring the Magic: Once we have passed through the threshold of the High Priestess's temple, we arrive in the fertile lands of the Empress. The Empress has walked through the mysteries of the Priestess and now sits upon her throne to observe the world around her. She is sovereign over her land, possessing the power to make choices, lending her support as she chooses, and celebrating all forms of creation and existence. The Empress is the Creatrix, a pyramid of life and a nexus of creation. She nurtures creativity, represents fertility, and promotes abundance. There are few rules here, except respecting the art of creation itself.

Three has a solid reputation for being a sacred number across numerous cultures for thousands of years. There are the three Cauldrons of Poesy, deities represented as trinities, and the idea of a three-part soul, not to mention the fact that we are often considering the threefold concepts of mind, body, and spirit and past, present, and future. Each of these concepts represents choices and viewpoints that make up a greater whole. When these threefold wisdoms are recognized and utilized in practice, we often experience growth ourselves. Three is a natural number of abundance—when two combine, a third comes into being.

Three is also the proverbial fork in the road. You can choose to split off to the right or the left or even go back the way you came if that's an option. Some may even say you could choose to go off-roading and make your own path. That's the power of choice—when you are thinking creatively, you might realize that the correct choice is not one that is immediately presented in front of you, but something you must build on your own.

The Empress asks us: Do we rely solely on what we already know, or do we allow ourselves to become creative, to take risks and discover our power of creation? Creativity feeds our imagination—something that is often underrated in today's society. When we allow ourselves to play, to express ourselves artistically and support others in creative pursuits, we become better problem-solvers and communicators. Our empathy and understanding deepen, while our capacity to connect with others magnifies. Will we hold onto our sovereignty or hand it over to someone else? One more lesson from the Empress: We don't have to say yes to everything and everyone in order to be creative. We must remember to take care of ourselves in order to keep the creativity flowing. We honor the creative and intuitive parts of ourselves when we learn to recognize our own power and protect it when needed.

Put It in Motion: From a seated or standing position, raise your arms above you, palms flat, with fingertips meeting to form a point above your head. Bring your arms down and apart, until they are fully extended out at your sides, describing the sides of a pyramid. Complete the base of the triangle by bringing your hands in to meet at your navel. Inhale and exhale. Reverse direction and repeat at least three times.

The Emperor

The Number: 4

The Shape: Square, rectangle, diamond

Snapshot: A crowned and armored figure sits squarely upon a throne, gazing steadily forward.

Musing: *Standing on the shoulders of giants.*

Core Principles: Foundation, structure, what we build upon for security, founding principles and guidelines, leadership

Add It Up: Four is the core number of quadrilaterals, which include squares, diamonds, and rectangles. Each of these polygons is formed by two intersecting pairs of parallel lines. This layering or weaving of parallel and perpendicular lines creates a stable structure and foundational form that is clearly defined.

As children, we often play with blocks, learning how to build (and break down) on a small and safe scale. We know that houses can be made of bricks—squares and rectangles stacked on a foundation to create a structure we can live within. And even though we think of a pyramid as a triangle—which it does form in silhouette—a traditional pyramid has a square for its foundation and 4 sides that angle upward. Four makes a simple yet solid base for building and delineating space.

One way to arrive at 4 is through this equation:

Magician: Building Skills & Experience (1) + Empress: Creativity & Choices (3) = Emperor: Foundation & Structure (4)

When we add the skills and learned experience of the Magician with the Empress's creativity and empowerment, we can form a solid foundation to build upon and guide by.

But that's not the only way to get to 4. Not only does 2 + 2 = 4, but so does 2 × 2 = 4. Either combination gets us to the stability of 4. Consider the High Priestess in conversation with herself or squared energetically. Remember those two pillars? Add another set and you have the potential for a temple with a floor and a roof. We have learned to balance the dualities and build upon them to create structure.

Exploring the Magic: Situated at 4, the Emperor aids in building a foundation that provides guidance, rules, and security for the creative ideas and abundance gifted by the Empress. The number 4 relates to balance and foundation, which is embodied in the Emperor's characteristics of being a leader and an authority figure. The Emperor holds wisdom from the past and reminds you to observe traditions and call upon your learned experiences—but don't find yourself beholden to them without reason or question. The Emperor can also protect you without confining you, giving you guidance and support that enables growth.

Structure and rules may seem contrary to creativity, abundance, and sovereignty, but they're not always at odds. Take a garden, for instance. If you want to grow a lot of tomatoes, it's recommended to provide plants with sturdy cages that help them support the weight of their fruit. Otherwise the plant may collapse under its own weight. Careful pruning can help prevent disease and encourage even more growth. We may be a bit more complicated than plants, but being given support, guidance, and routine care does make a world of difference. Overbearing structure, strict guidelines, and overprotection can inhibit growth, so we don't want the box of safety and security to become a prison. Be guided but not stifled.

We also find the number 4 in structural applications of magic. Many magical practitioners talk about four elements—Air, Fire, Water, and Earth—as the foundation for physical life and creation. There are the four suits of the Minor Arcana, relating back to the elements, which we will explore more in chapter 5. There are also the four cardinal directions—north, south, east, and west—which create the foundation of the compass rose. I often joke that while folks talk about casting a circle, we're often casting a magic square or diamond instead. We can see all these applications as the realm of the Emperor, helping to create form and guidance for our goals.

Put It in Motion: As we typically think of a foundation as being on the floor, this exercise is going to start with your feet. Stand with your feet just about shoulder width apart. Extend your arms straight up, above your head. You are framing a rectangle: foot to hand, hand to hand, hand to foot, and foot to foot. Feel the strength of this position, connecting ground to sky. If you'd like, you can also do a box turn in a count of four steps to feel the shape in all directions. For a more stationary option, in a sturdy chair, copy the symmetrical sitting position modeled by the Emperor: feet squarely on the floor, arms out at your sides.

The Hierophant

The Number: *5*

The Shape: Pentagram, pentacle, pentagon

Snapshot: A pope-like figure sits on a throne, hands raised in benediction. Two acolytes look up at the figure from a step below the throne.

Musing: *I am the house ruled by spirit.*

Core Principles: Cycles and circles, spiritual doctrine, legacy and tradition, hierarchy

Add It Up: The pentagon, pentagram, and pentacle are all shapes based on the number 5. Whereas 4 feels solid, almost sedentary, with its shapes, especially squares and rectangles, 5's shapes tend to have a sense of motion to them. There is a variation of a pentagon that is more like a square with a triangle for a hat (versus the equilateral pentagon), which gives the impression of a house or a church, connecting the physical with the spiritual. The other 5-based shapes, like the equilateral pentagon, the pentagram, and the pentacle, all feel like they could start rolling at any moment.

Here are some equations that bring us to 5:

High Priestess: Communication & Exploring the Mystery (2) + Empress: Creativity & Choices (3) = Hierophant: Spiritual Legacy (5)

Magician: Building Skills & Experience (1) + Emperor: Foundation & Structure (4) = Hierophant: Spiritual Legacy (5)

These two equations are fascinating when we look at the traditionally assigned gender presentation of the cards, where one set is feminine and the other is masculine. One might see them as equations that result in a matriarchal Hierophant versus a patriarchal Hierophant. The reality is that we are not stuck with the gender binary and the roots of *all* these cards are a blending of presentations. But let's entertain the difference in energies for a moment and consider what they have to do with the cyclical nature of the Hierophant, as the pendulum swings from one extreme to the other.

Our first equation (2 + 3 = 5) combines the High Priestess and the Empress to arrive at the Hierophant. This version of the Hierophant may be more intuitive, supportive, and creative in nature, resulting in a more democratic assembly fostered by discussion and individual expression. As the organization is more free-form and mystery is celebrated, boundaries could be blurred or ignored and rules might be misinterpreted or overlooked.

Our second equation (1 + 4 = 5) combines the Magician and the Emperor, emphasizing skill, mastery, structure, and rules. Everything may be out in the open, but there's little room for creativity or mystery. Hard edges and precision are the spiritual center, mandating conformity and correctness. This view prohibits thinking outside the box and demands that we discard anything out of the ordinary, stifling creativity and individualism.

Each equation shows us something in this incarnation that both works *and* can go awry. Sometimes we need more transparency and structure with our beliefs, and sometimes we need to be more open to change and breaking the rules.

Exploring the Magic: The Emperor gave you the structure and foundation to support your skills, sovereignty, and creativity in the physical realm of Earth, Air, Fire, and Water. Now the fifth element emerges with the Hierophant: Spirit. Hence, "I am the house ruled by spirit" presents the insight that our bodies are the houses ruled by us—the embodied spirits." We are the pentagram—all the elements united and awakened.

The Hierophant is a teacher bringing spiritual guidance and direction, reminding us of the metaphysical and symbolic tools that await our direction. Depending on where we are in our development, we either yearn for the spiritual teachings of the Hierophant or wish to rebel against them.

Why is 5 a cycle and what does that have to do with spirituality? I think that in humanity's development, we find a repeating pattern when it comes to civilization and religion. First we figure out the how and why to do a thing, then we began to contextualize what deeper meaning it can possess, connecting it to religion or spirituality. Then we question those spiritual and religious meanings and resolve to go back to the roots of how and why. Repeat.

The challenge of the Hierophant is to evaluate our spiritual traditions and beliefs. We must contemplate which ideas and beliefs still serve us and will continue on and what others are harmful and need to be discarded.

Put It in Motion: To connect with the energy of the Hierophant, we will make our whole body the pentagram. Either standing or lying down, spread out your arms and legs. Your head combined with your limbs make the whole of the star. Close your eyes and extend out as far as you can reach. Take a deep breath in and then exhale. Feel the expansiveness and power of this pose, then gently bring your arms and legs back to your sides.

The Lovers

The Number: 6

The Shape: Hexagon, hexagram

Snapshot: A pair of naked figures flank a centralized angelic being who bestows a gesture of blessing.

Musing: *What sets your heart in motion?*

Core Principles: Motion, passion, partnerships and unions

Add It Up: Six is a pretty sexy and vibrant number that just seems to have a hum to it. Perhaps that's because honeycombs are hexagons. Hexagrams also represent a merger of complementary worlds—above and below, within and without. As things just seem to want to come together so well at 6, it's no wonder the Lovers card is set here.

Our equations:

Emperor: Foundation & Structure (4) + High Priestess: Communication & Exploring the Mystery (2) = The Lovers: What Moves Us (6)

When a solid structure and safe place meet a willingness to explore, we get the combination of right place, right time = destiny.

Hierophant: Spiritual Legacy (5) + Magician: Building Skills & Experience (1) = The Lovers: What Moves Us (6)

This equation represents a passion for vocation and learning more so than romantic love.

High Priestess: Communication & Exploring the Mystery (2) × Empress: Creativity & Choices (3) = The Lovers: What Moves Us (6)

Open communication that allows us to discuss hopes and fears magnified by support and informed consent is a recipe that fosters passionate hearts.

Exploring the Magic: The Lovers signify passion, harmony, love, attraction, motion, and unions. This card is a reminder to be human and honor that for all it entails. We are physically embodied spirits, which is something to be celebrated. Rather than separating everything into vice or virtue, sacred or profane, we can choose to fall in love with the magical, physical body and the harmony of inner and outer lives interwoven. We can see the beauty of romance in all its forms, enjoy sex or refrain, appreciate lust or harness desire—all the while practicing respect and consent.

The question asked here is: What moves your heart? Or, perhaps, what will complete it? The mysterious dualities we questioned with the High Priestess are now fully present and moving together harmoniously. True love, passionate encounters, companionship, partnership—all in creative abundance with endless possibilities in this moment.

The Lovers card isn't just about relationships with others; it can be about self-love and developing a more passionate bond with yourself. This card can be a reminder to respect and understand yourself fully, to set your own rules and values by the beat of your heart. The Emperor and the Hierophant may have given you rules, but the thing about rules is that they are made to be broken—especially when they don't embrace the whole of the self in a healthy way. You must sort out where the truth lies for you and what sets your heart free. It is an act of revolution to believe in yourself. To believe in the power and beauty of your own body is a riot and an act of radical self-love.

When we embrace the 6 energy of the hexagram, we can find the balance between our symbolic bodies and our earthly ones. In that liminal space, we find love where sky and earth do meet, aligned with our hearts.

Put It in Motion: While the hexagon and hexagram are the shapes that best represent the energy of the Lovers (and you should practice drawing them!), this movement exercise focuses on the heart. You can be seated or stand. Extend your arms up just above your head and slightly out. Take a deep breath in and move your hands down diagonally to meet at your heart and exhale. With your hands still resting at your heart, inhale again. As you exhale, move your hands and arms down and out past your hips. Repeat this gesture three times. The overall shape of both motions makes an X over your torso, describing the energetic feel of the hexagram without being an exact trace. You're connecting your heart to above and below, within and without.

The Chariot

The Number: 7

The Shape: Septagon, septagram

Snapshot: A charioteer faces the viewer directly on. Their cart is pulled by two beasts, one black and one white.

Musing: *Full speed ahead!*

Core Principles: Pursuit, unified action, momentum, triumph, navigation

Add It Up: With so many sides and points, the septagon and septagram seem ready to roll and spin on their own, making fairly functional wheels for the Chariot while acting as a charm of protection. It's not the smoothest ride, but once you get going, you get used to it!

Each of our equations helps determine what drives the Chariot forward and hopefully hints at what direction it's heading in:

Empress: Creativity & Choices (3) + Emperor: Foundation & Structure (4) = Chariot: Forward Motion (7)

With the abundant energy of the Empress and the framework and guidelines of the Emperor, the Chariot has both momentum and a track to run on. This is a good pairing for business.

Hierophant: Spiritual Legacy (5) + High Priestess: Communication & Exploring the Mystery (2) = Chariot: Forward Motion (7)

This equation indicates spiritual vocation. The querent is on a spiritual quest, directed by forces perhaps much greater than themselves. They may not fully understand why, but they know they are driven nonetheless and determined.

The Lovers: What Moves Us (6) + Magician: Building Skills & Experience (1) = Chariot: Forward Motion (7)

With hearts set ablaze and a willingness to experiment powered by confidence, passion sets the pace for this race.

Exploring the Magic: The Chariot represents forward movement—motivated by the passion of the Lovers. As things speed up, it takes more focus and will to help steer in the direction you wish to go. There are obstacles, competition, and other kinds of opposing forces to contend with.

The Lovers have helped you learn about creating harmony, celebrating your passion, and getting inspired for the next step. The Chariot asks you to get in and go—putting ideas in practice to achieve balance. Seven is an especially powerful number of manifestation. It may seem strange that an odd-numbered card would represent balance, but balance isn't static, it's dynamic. Balance is about creating union between opposites and making unifying actions.

Movement can be scary. You may be afraid that you might lose control or be judged. What if you think you have two left feet or always seem to be dropping things? The Chariot reminds you that these fearful obstacles can be overcome through determination, focus, and willpower. Just be sure to focus on the road ahead of you and remember the goals that drive you.

Put It in Motion: For the Chariot, we are going to take the V-like motion we made with the Lovers card, and instead of directing it up or down, we are going to push it out directly in front of us, in all four directions. Face east and make a V with your hands in front of your heart (fingertips facing front). Then push out in front of you, tracing a larger V. Once your arms are fully extended, relax them back down to your sides. Turn to the south and repeat the gesture. Repeat again in the west and north until you are back to facing east. With this gesture, you are sending your heart out, clearing the path in front of you in all directions.

Strength

The Number: 8

The Shape: Figure eight, infinity, lemniscate

Snapshot: A calm figure holds the jaws of a lion shut with little feeling of struggle or strife.

Musing: *Be the body united—mind, body, and spirit.*

Core Principles: Cohesion, unification of physical and metaphysical strengths, alignment, applied wisdom

Add It Up: A figure eight is an endless, fluid loop of energy that exemplifies the stable nature and calming qualities of this card. Depending on its orientation, the energy moves either side to side or up and down—balancing the hemispheres of the brain, above and below. While 8 is 4 doubled, we don't see the pointy corners of the square or rectangle here. Strength comes not in the form of 90-degree angles but rather with flexible curves. This truth helps us challenge our core ideas of what strength really is and where it actually comes from.

The following equations pinpoint how we can build up our strengths:

Hierophant: Spiritual Legacy (5) + Empress: Creativity & Choices (3) = Strength: Mind, Body, Spirit (8)

Here we are learning about respecting our spiritual needs while validating our bodily autonomy. The spirit supports the body and vice versa, creating a healthy balance and energetic exchange.

The Lovers: What Moves Us (6) + High Priestess: Communication & Exploring the Mystery (2) = Strength: Mind, Body, Spirit (8)

We find strength by loving our bodies and celebrating what makes us each unique while being conscious of our weaknesses. By acknowledging where we need support, we can overcome what holds us back.

Chariot: Forward Motion (7) + Magician: Building Skills & Experience (1) = Strength: Mind, Body, Spirit (8)

This combination challenges us to ask if we have gotten too comfortable or if we are challenging ourselves by learning or trying something new. Are we ready to see how far we can go if we try?

Emperor: Foundation & Structure (4) × High Priestess: Communication & Exploring the Mystery (2) = Strength: Mind, Body, Spirit (8)

Are we providing ourselves with the best routine and guidelines to help us build, or do we fear failure and therefore don't even try?

Exploring the Magic: Strength signifies being able to release your fears so that you can unite your mind, body, and soul. It speaks of physical strength combined and enhanced with emotional and mental strength. Strength embodies the triumph of love over hate. Eight, with its relation to the ever-looping infinity, brings us mastery and serenity.

Our time spent with the Chariot involved action in motion, striving to achieve balance between multiple (often opposing) factors. The pursuing nature of 7 requires thinking on your feet, allowing yourself to shift ideas and plans on the fly in order to keep the momentum going.

As we move into the Strength card, we balance the physicality of instinct and reflex with the wisdom of intuition and forethought. We are learning to confront our fears using our gained experience and critical thinking. Practicing calm in the face of adversity, we gather the courage to do what we know is right in both our hearts and minds.

In contrast to the motion of the Chariot, we recognize that within Strength is the knowledge that sometimes stillness is the best course of action. It teaches us to hold fast, to contemplate, to allow ourselves time to listen, observe, and absorb the world around us. We begin to recognize that rest can be just as sacred as activity—as well as understanding the necessary balance of both in our lives. The lion represents our primal self, raw physicality, and impulsiveness—tempered by reason, experience, and focus. This is all done with feet firmly on the ground, standing connected to the earth.

Put It in Motion: I love teaching figure eights in dance because they're so powerful and yet so calming and entrancing. Depending on your comfort level and flexibility, you can start by simply tracing a figure eight with your finger—either in the air or on a surface. As you loosen up, try using the range of your whole arm, then both arms moving together. Explore all the different ways you can draw a figure eight with your body. How does each feel?

The Hermit

The Number: 9

The Shape: Enneagon, nonagon

Snapshot: A lone cloaked figure with a staff holds a lantern aloft.

Musing: *There is illumination in the darkness—and snacks!*

Core Principles: Introspection, guidance, searching, rejuvenation

Add It Up: If you squint at the enneagon (nine-sided figure), you might think it's a circle. That's how close we are to finishing up this first cycle as we stop and chill with the Hermit.

These equations help us determine what we need to be introspective about, what has led us to the Hermit's door:

Emperor: Foundation & Structure (4) + Hierophant: Spiritual Legacy (5) = Hermit: Introspection (9)

Is the structure solid? Is this legacy something we wish to continue building or exploring?

The Lovers: What Moves Us (6) + Empress: Creativity & Choices (3) = Hermit: Introspection (9)

We've been swept up by passion and everything is moving so fast that it may be wise to take a break.

Chariot: Forward Motion (7) + High Priestess: Communication & Exploring the Mystery (2) = Hermit: Introspection (9)

Your higher self is saying, "I think we've been here already. Better stop and check for directions."

Strength: Mind, Body, Spirit (8) + Magician: Building Skills & Experience (1) = Hermit: Introspection (9)

At this point in the journey, we're doing good, but it's to freshen up on some old lessons and go over the basics to make sure we've still got what we think we need.

Exploring the Magic: The Hermit beckons us to enter, take a load off, refresh, and contemplate both the journey we've been through and what's next to come. A hermitage is a place where the hermit (or a collective group of like-minded individuals) lives in seclusion from the world, retreating from the outside to contemplate the inner worlds—another duality.

In the cave of the Hermit, you will find that body, mind, and spirit have been balanced within and without, thanks to Strength. The Hermit never retreats into their cave unprepared; they take exactly what they need with them to sustain them and prepare them for future mysteries. This is why I like to say that the Hermit always has snacks. You just know they do.

In the RWS card, a figure holds up a lantern lit by a 6-pointed star (Love), guiding the way. The way the lantern is held aloft (while the Hermit gazes downward) gives us the sense that they are holding the light not only for themselves but also for someone else to see—a beacon in the darkness. So while the Hermit represents introspection and quietude, we recognize that there is the guide and the guided. The Hermit is lighting the way for us to the hermitage, a sanctuary for exploration and consideration.

The Hermit, at number 9, is also the Empress threefold. We see within this card the opportunity for abundance, creativity, and exploring options, but there is also a reminder of the sanctity of sovereignty, of taking care of the self and protecting your light. In this case, being "selfish" is not a negative thing, but a necessary one. In order to help others, we must tend to ourselves in preparation. Accepting assistance when it is needed is never weakness. Rather, it speaks of courage, maturity, and strength of character, so that in the future, when we are ready, we too can hold our lantern aloft and be a guide to others.

Put It in Motion: To recognize ourselves mind, body, and spirit and align our inner cauldrons, we are going to acknowledge our head, heart, and belly. Sitting or standing, with both hands, bring your fingertips to your forehead, then your sternum, and finally your navel. Repeat two more times (for a total of three passes).

The Wheel of Fortune

The Number: 10

The Shape: Circle, wheel

Snapshot: A great wheel, full of symbols, spins in the heavens.

Musing: *Take another turn at the wheel.*

Core Principles: Cycle of fate, starting/ending cycles, completion, a turn of fortune, opportunity, hope

Add It Up: We've arrived at our first double-digit number, 10. If we combine its base numbers of 1 + 0, we find the Magician. The Magician reminds us of what we have learned and experienced in this past cycle. With the essence of 0 and the Fool, not only are we beginning again in a new way, but we should also hold onto that sense of wonder, to seek joy in the world and foster happiness.

As you look at the possible equations, consider what factors and qualities from the prior cards got you to this point. You're now familiar with each of these cards, so I encourage you to contemplate what each pairing means to you.

6 + 4 = 10: The Lovers: What Moves Us (6) + Emperor: Foundation & Structure (4)

Congratulations! Following your passion and sticking to your principles has given you a solid foundation that also satisfies your heart's desire. You are doing what you love and feeling the support all around.

7 + 3 = 10: Chariot: Forward Motion (7) + Empress: Creativity & Choices (3)

Being relentless in the pursuit of your goals and not compromising your power has led to success in achieving them. The experience may have been a bit messy at times, but you learned a lot for the next round.

8 + 2 = 10: Strength: Mind, Body, Spirit (8) + High Priestess: Communication & Exploring the Mystery (2)

Hard work has paid off. You might not know what your next step is, but trust that you are on the right path for now.

9 + 1 = 10: Hermit: Introspection (9) + Magician: Building Skills & Experience (1)

Trust in your own abilities has led you to become adept and achieve your goals. The journey may have been lonely at times, but the sacrifice feels well worth it.

5 × 2 = 10: Hierophant: Spiritual Legacy (5) × High Priestess: Communication & Exploring the Mystery (2)

Back at the Chariot, these two cards added up to indicate a spiritual quest. Here we are magnifying them with multiplication, which essentially accelerates their energy. With the result of 10, there is a sense of completing that quest, becoming ordained or sanctified in some way, ready now to be in the service of others.

Exploring the Magic: At 10, the Wheel of Fortune indicates the completion of a cycle—which also means we're about to start another one. Even if things didn't work out exactly as we'd hoped, here's an opportunity to try again. The 0 in 10 reminds us that the Fool is still with us, inside. The Fool says it's not a bad thing to have a beginner's mind or a hopeful outlook. In fact, these traits may save you down the road.

When I look at the Wheel of Fortune card, I am reminded of the song by Inkubus Sukkubus called "Craft of the Wise," which references a wheel that spins forever around. If you aren't familiar with the song or this English goth/pagan rock band, you might assume they're referencing the Wheel of the Year, which is a pretty good guess. But the reference has to do more with the cycles of life and civilization itself, patterns of both growth and destruction.

The turn of the wheel might feel like both a blessing and a curse, but this flow is the truth that is the rhythm of the universe. Everything in this world has a start and a finish; all things destroyed become new things assembled in a different way. We are all made of star-stuff, spirit in the guise of the universe dreaming itself together and apart. As they say, the only real constant is change.

Whether this turn at the wheel brings joy or sadness, it's an opportunity to learn. Also, you're at the wheel, so where you take this ride depends on you. Be open to the possibilities, find your center, and move in a way that follows the beat of your heart.

Put It in Motion: To fully experience the Wheel of Fortune, it's now time to do a cartwheel—just kidding! (Unless you're a gymnast—then please by all means do.) For this exercise, stand centered and extend your arms out, palms facing up. Slowly turn clockwise for one revolution, then reverse and turn counterclockwise. You can do multiple revolutions in each direction if you'd like, as long as you don't get dizzy. Another option is to sit in a chair that spins and perform the same motion. Feel the openness of the movement, the connection to the world around you, the motion of the wheel as it turns with you as the center.

———— •●• ————

Congratulations! Not only have you reached the end of the first half of the Major Arcana, but it's also the end of this chapter. Before moving on to the next chapter, I recommend taking a little break and sitting with these 11 cards. What new things have you learned about them? How do they make you feel? Is there a particular card that stands out to you as relevant right in this moment? Put it aside or make a note—and when you're ready, turn the page.

CHAPTER 4

The Major Arcana—from 11 to 21

As there are 22 Major Arcana, if we split the cards down the middle, we get 11 in the first set and 11 in the second set. We see symmetry at work, and it feels appropriate that Justice aligns with 11 and starts off our second set of Major Arcana cards.

The first half of the Major Arcana largely describes the internal journey, tying into who we are becoming and how we will work through that. After we reach the Wheel of Fortune, the second half of the Major Arcana focuses more on external influences and experiences that challenge what we've built internally. These 11 cards put us in context with the world—what's happening to us in these situations, where are we in them, and how does that change us?

We will be exploring this second part of the Major Arcana a little differently than we did the first. The "Add It Up" section includes a list of the possible arithmetic operations that can make up the card. As we saw in the first section, these combinations by addition and multiplication help us arrive at the card we're examining. Instead of breaking down every single possible combination (the higher the card number, the more possibilities), a few key examples are highlighted. I encourage you to consider the other combinations through journaling as you make notes on each card.

What's also different in the second part is that our shapes are becoming more symbolic and representative as the numbers increase, as it doesn't do much good to try and connect with a 17-sided polygon. The associated shapes still contain energy of the card, but on a more complex level.

There's a new section in this chapter called "Inner Math." This breaks down the card number itself to reveal some more insight. We will look at what happens when we add both digits together and we multiply them together.

$(1 + X = Y)$—By adding the card numbers up, Y indicates what we hope to accomplish in the future as we take with us the lessons from this particular card.

$(1 \times X = X)$—When we multiply the card's digits together, it reveals what we should remember from our past experiences in order to best work with this card.

Obviously, for the Judgement (20) and World (21) cards, 1 is replaced by 2 in the equation, but the format is still effective for the addition and multiplication variations.

Lastly, the "Put It in Motion" section isn't present, as the movement exploration for many of these shapes can get too complicated to put into words easily. Instead, I recommend that you take the suggested shape and use it as a drawing exercise. Doodle it, trace it repeatedly, or do whatever helps you feel the energy of the shape through your hand.[19] If you'd like to work with your whole body, you can also examine the activity happening in your cards and practice those poses and motions with your body.

You can also take the movements from the first group of Major Arcana and add the shape of the card to play with. For example, with Temperance (14), you could assume the squared-off seated position from the Emperor (4) and use both arms to trace mirrored spirals in front of you. You could also use the equations as guidance for putting together movements, creating a moving meditation that reflects the combined card.

Remember in the last chapter when I asked if a particular card was standing out to you? See where it shows up in this next chapter and how it factors into our second set of Major Arcana cards.

Let us continue into the mysteries.

19. For a more in-depth exploration of shapes and movements, I recommend playing with my Sigil Witchery Oracle. With it, you can discover a large variety of shapes, marks, and symbols—and multiple ways to work with them beyond sigils!

Justice

The Number: 11

The Shape: Scales

Snapshot: A stately robed figure sits between two pillars, holding a sword aloft in one hand and a set of scales in the other.

Musing: *Balance is dynamic, not static.*

Core Principles: Balancing effort, understanding complex duality, truth revealed, cause and effect

Add It Up: Eleven may be an odd number, but it sure is even in presentation and feels balanced. Many people associate 11 with spiritual concepts and connection, even if they don't consider themselves to be particularly spiritual. The number and variety of people who remark on seeing 11:11 on a digital clock is rather staggering. There's just something about it that feels like a message from someone or somewhere, just for us.

Possible equations: 1 + 10, 2 + 9, 3 + 8, 4 + 7, 5 + 6

9 + 2 = 11: High Priestess: Communication & Exploring the Mystery (2) + Hermit: Introspection (9) = Justice (11)

We will know the truth of our hearts by taking responsibility for our actions. We can be a guide or model for others if we are honest with ourselves and focus on what's right and just.

Inner Math:

(1 + 1 = 2, High Priestess)—To overcome fears and find balance

(1 × 1 = 1, Magician)—Lean into skills and experience in order to persevere.

Exploring the Magic: Justice is a formidable card that is up-front about what it means—truth in advertising, as it's said. The energy of the Justice card emphasizes the search for balance and truth, the need to deliver fair and just results, and the revelation of experiencing the consequences and/or rewards of one's actions. We see the scales being balanced and the sword of action is held and ready to deliver or defend justice. The sword isn't necessarily bringing punishment, but clarity, as it clears away what's not needed and exposes the truth.

Even though the figure in the RWS is seated, there's a hint of a foot peeking out from the hem of the robe. This suggests to me that Justice isn't going to sit around either—Justice can spring into action at any moment.

It's not surprising to me that the digits in 11 can be added together to make 2, as this card clearly references the High Priestess. We see two pillars, though in this instance they match. A curtain hangs behind the seated figure. We know what we've done to get here. There's no mystery to it.

Justice's placement after 10 is no mistake either.[20] A new cycle begins and we must deal with both the positive and the negative results of the previous cycle. As the Magician (1 + 0 = 1), these results are the tools sitting on our table. Once again, we are challenged not only to look at what's in front of us or put it on display as a badge but also to consider what we are going to *do* about it.

20. Strength at 8 and Justice at 11 has always made sense to me, especially when you consider Strength as an internal/personal development card and Justice as an external/in the environment card. However, you will find these card placements reversed in the Marseille and Thoth decks. Arthur Waite may have switched them to align with the Golden Dawn's astrological associations, but symbolically and energetically I think it works as well.

The Hanged One

The Number: 12

The Shape: Tree or T-shaped cross

Snapshot: A figure with their hands bound behind their back hangs upside down from one leg.

Musing: *Sacrifice brings release.*

Core Principles: On hold, sacrifices, suspension

Add It Up: We find 12 all around us: 12 months in our calendar year, 12 zodiac signs, 12 hours per period of the day and on the clock. We start to feel time's grip on us and feel stuck or overwhelmed, unable to change anything. But when we break 12 down, we can regain perspective and find that our rhythm doesn't have to be controlled by the ticktock of the clock.

Possible equations: 7 + 5, 8 + 4, 9 + 3, 10 + 2, 11 + 1, 6 × 2, 3 × 4

2 × 6 = 12: High Priestess: Communication & Exploring the Mystery (2) × The Lovers: What Moves Us (6) = The Hanged One (12)

When we remember what moves us, what our passion is, and overcome our fears, we can move with power to the next stage of growth. More will be revealed through sacrifice.

Inner Math:

(1 + 2 = 3, Empress)—To be fruitful, abundant, and in control

(1 × 2 = 2, High Priestess)—Release fear, be bold, regain perspective.

Exploring the Magic: Now we have arrived at the Hanged One (12). This can be a frustrating and seemingly difficult card to encounter, especially after we've just tapped into the flow of the Wheel and experienced the focus of the Justice card. Now it seems like we could be stuck. But once we move past our initial frustration, we find that our practice is enhanced by exercising patience. The lessons the Hanged One brings include suspending our activities to seek wisdom and the realization that sometimes we must make a sacrifice to become unstuck.

Remember that 12 can be the Lovers multiplied by the High Priestess. Rather than focus on the lack of movement or progress you're seeing on the outside, take this time to turn inward. Refamiliarize yourself with your goals and what sets your heart ablaze. Tune into your body and pay attention to the signs it is sending you. Listen, sit with the feelings, acknowledge the aches and the urges. What are the potential fears and barriers that are holding you back? What is the best move forward?

The Hanged One is often related to sacrifice, especially when aligned with the story of Odin hanging from the World Tree in order to gain the wisdom of the runes. Making a sacrifice is typically seen as giving up, losing, or destroying something, usually for the sake of something else. But *sacrifice* shares a root with the word *sacred*, and the transfer of energy itself is sacred. Practicing patience often involves sacrificing our time so that we may arrive at a better outcome, receive wisdom, or allow for the path ahead to clear. While we may lose time or experience some other kind of loss, we gain much more in exchange for that sacrifice—finding ourselves even more whole and empowered. So what might seem like a loss or an obstacle suddenly transforms into something very worthy and beyond our initial fathoming.

Death

The Number: 13

The Shape: Wavy line

Snapshot: An apparition of Death as a knight on a white horse moves toward the future.

Musing: *Death is not an end, but a transition.*

Core Principles: Change after sacrifice, regeneration, necessary clearing, transformation

Add It Up: Many people seem to think that 13 is an unlucky number, but it's a special and lucky number for me. (I was born on the 13th.) I find that many magical folks also feel the same way. While the general population may not be too fond of 13—and it being paired with Death in this card doesn't help much with that—I think this discomfort also says something about modern society's relationship with death as a whole. Our current culture doesn't have the healthiest relationship with birth *or* death. We prefer to ignore these important parts of life, sanitizing them or hiding them away, locking away the key to our human mysteries. When we face these life phases, we can live more fully and honor life as we should.

We have quite a few interesting equations to consider that add up to 13:

1 + 12: The Magician + The Hanged Man

Using our skills to move forward after change.

2 + 11: The High Priestess + Justice

Power and balance prevail over fear of the unknown.

3 + 10: The Empress + Wheel of Fortune

Creativity brings a new cycle and capacity for growth.

4 + 9: The Emperor + The Hermit

Use introspection to formulate new foundation concepts.

5 + 8: The Hierophant + Strength

Spirituality combined with wisdom of the heart and mind.

6 + 7: The Lovers + The Chariot

Celebrate being embodied, revel in the moment, because tomorrow is never promised.

Inner Math:

(1 + 3 = 4, Emperor)—Regain stability, a sense of purpose

(1 × 3 = 3, Empress)—Compassion, the ability to change and be flexible, to recreate ourselves

Exploring the Magic: Death signifies the change and renewal that comes after sacrifice. The Hanged One taught us about patience, sacrifice in its many forms, paying attention even when we're frustrated, and the power of release. That release means we're able to transform and move forward with the aid of the Death card.

When examining this card closely, one of the first things I notice is that Death and their horse are moving forward into the future. Yes, Death is ever present, but it is also clearly not an ending. This truth is echoed in the placement of the card at 13. It's not at the end of the Major Arcana, but somewhat in the middle—so there's much more traveling and transformation ahead!

We also see the pomegranate flower prominently displayed on the flag, which harkens back to the High Priestess. (The flag is also blowing forward into the future.) It is a sign not to fear the unknown. Instead, delve deeper into the mysteries, as we carry them with us always. These mysteries are constantly unfolding within us, seeds ready to take root and begin another cycle of life.

If we take the fallen figure with the overturned crown to represent a king or emperor energy, then Death is telling us to allow our ideals and foundational concepts to transform: to allow ourselves to transform by not holding on so tightly to that which no longer serves us.

While not physically depicted in the card included here, the Death card holds tremendous serpent energy: the ability to renew oneself, to change course as needed, to move in liminal spaces, traversing both underworlds and the worlds above. This motion is one of the reasons the shape for this card is the wavy line—symbolizing the ever-flowing undulations of the serpent, with its ability to transform and renew itself by shedding its skin. We, too, must be willing to shed our skins when the time calls for it.

Temperance

The Number: 14

The Shape: Spiral (in and out)

Snapshot: A winged figure stands on the edge of a pond, pouring water between two cups.

Musing: *Everything in moderation.*

Core Principles: Regaining balance, equilibrium, give-and-take, moderation

Add It Up: When teaching my Sigil Witchery workshop, I often make the joke that all numbers are magical—except 14. This usually stuns people for a moment until I let them know I'm kidding. (Every number is magical, because math!) The number 14 often gets overlooked in the Tarot because folks think that Temperance is just this nice, calm card that tells you to do "everything in moderation," but there's so much more to 14 and Temperance than that. Oscar Wilde is credited with saying "Everything in moderation, including moderation"—so remember that balance isn't static; it's all about quality of motion.

Possible equations: $6 + 8$, $5 + 9$, $4 + 10$, $3 + 11$, $2 + 12$, $1 + 13$, 7×2

7 × 2 = 14: Chariot: Forward Motion (7) + High Priestess: Communication & Exploring the Mystery (2) = Temperance (14)

Things are moving fast. We may feel like we are a mystery in motion, but following our intuition will sharpen our focus and keep us balanced.

10 + 4 = 14: Wheel of Fortune: Change (10) + Emperor: Foundation & Structure (4) = Temperance (14)

Change can be disorienting. To regain focus, find your footing by focusing on building structure and setting guidelines in your agenda. Take your time and double-check your calculations before making any decisions.

Inner Math:

($1 + 4 = 5$, Hierophant)—To establish a spiritual legacy, release ego and the need to control everything.

($1 \times 4 = 4$, Emperor)—Remember your roots, find your footing, build with care.

Exploring the Magic: Temperance is all about regaining balance and momentum while rebuilding your core beliefs. It's no surprise that the root of 14 is 7, referencing the Chariot. It's time to spiral back to our center and remember who we are, then spiral our way back out into the world.

We have experienced the transformation of the Death card. Now it is time to stand with the Temperance card and find our footing again. Normally I would say to "sit" with a card, but this is a clue that the energy of the Temperance card is more active than passive. Yes, this card gives a sense of rest and recuperation from the energy of the Death card because, let's face it, even a welcomed transformation can be exhausting. But it's not exactly time for a break either. We need to keep our wits about us and be present and balanced, ready to move and to flow with what is needed.

Temperance feels very spiritual, with its angelic presence, calm demeanor, and Hierophant connection. But we're still embodied, living in the physical world. Even as we delve deeper into the spiritual realm, we are reminded to keep one foot in the physical realm, to keep ourselves grounded and remember the principles that form our foundation. We see this with the figure standing with one foot in the water and one on land as they pour the waters of life between two chalices. Those two chalices we also see in the 2 of Cups—a card focusing on relationships, emotional connection, and finding joy, balance, and kinship with like-minded souls. Passion from the Lovers and alignment from Strength can bring hope, courage, and renewed faith. Focus on the horizon, be brave and bold, listen to the voice within, and know that you are on the right path.

The Devil

The Number: 15

The Shape: Chain

Snapshot: A pair of loosely bound naked figures flank a large devil-like figure.

Musing: *What binds us can also set us free.*

Core Principles: Being held back, chained by old ideas or toxic habits, revelation of opportunities, recognizing resources, freedom, what needs to be released

Add It Up: The number 15 offers a lot of interesting combinations that aid us in digging into what the Devil has to say to us. In exploring 5 × 3 by referencing the shapes of the Hierophant (pentagram) and the Empress (triangle), we see that both shapes are present in the Devil card. First an inverted pentagram crowns the Devil—a call to look inside ourselves for spiritual guidance. The Devil with the two figures forms a triangle—our presence in this display is what feeds into this trapped energy. If we remove ourselves from the situation, the pattern will shift and the Devil will fall.

Possible equations: 1 + 14, 2 + 13, 3 + 12, 4 + 11, 5 + 10, 6 + 9, 7 + 8, 5 × 3

6 + 9 = 15: The Lovers: What Moves Us (6) + Hermit: Introspection (9) = The Devil (15)

Love is not shameful, our bodies are not shameful. Look inside and release the ideas that harm you and others. Be a beacon of change.

5 × 3 = 15: Hierophant: Spiritual Legacy (5) × Empress: Creativity & Choices (3) = The Devil (15)

Our desire to hold onto the past is limiting our powers of creation and our ability to engage freely in our future. We cannot be pinned down and fly freely at the same time.

Inner Math:

(1 + 5 = 6, Lovers)—If we let go of what holds us back, we can embrace more of what life has to offer in a healthier way.

(1 × 5 = 5, Hierophant)—Recognizing what no longer serves our spirit.

Exploring the Magic: With the Devil, we could find a message about leaning too hard into the physical realm to stabilize or insulate ourselves. But the Devil is far more metaphysical in nature. Here we are challenged to consider what is holding us back as well as what we are missing or ignoring. This card speaks to being chained down by toxic habits and concepts that are no longer healthy or relevant to us. These can be physical, emotional, or spiritual habits. There's also the potential for us to discover untapped resources and reconnect to the best parts of our human nature. The Devil is in the details really.

We're not really looking at the Devil here; we're seeing Baphomet, a figure found in multiple esoteric and occult traditions. Baphomet represents the mystical balance of opposites: masculine and feminine, primal and spiritual, positive and negative, chaos and order. My favorite representation of this card is in Legend: The Arthurian Tarot, where the Devil card shows the horned god, Cernunnos, as he's depicted on the Gundestrup Cauldron. It's a verdant card with rich greens and blues, showing Cernunnos in the middle of the woods, cool, calm, and collected. He seems to say, "Come, rewild yourself. Connect with your body so that you can rebalance your spirit. You have forgotten who you can be!"

Considering that the composition of the Devil card mirrors that of the Lovers card, the call to remember the beauty of being human and the passion of our hearts is spot-on. We've chained ideas to our bodies that hold us back from honoring life and each other. But the chains aren't permanent. They can be lifted off and we can walk away from that which appears to bind us. We're just so afraid that if we let go of these ideas, if we leave the institutions that confine us, then everything will fall and it will be our fault. But have you asked yourself, "How can I learn and move forward if I don't acknowledge my mistakes? What if it all *does* need to fall?"

The Tower

The Number: 16

The Shape: Zigzag

Snapshot: A tall tower is struck by lightning and is set ablaze while figures fall through the air.

Musing: *And so it all falls down. What's next?*

Core Principles: Cracked foundation, return to the roots, breakdown of unhealthy or languishing situations

Add It Up: We go from the unstable odd number of 15 to the nice and even 16, yet everything is falling around us. The interesting thing about 16 is that 4 is its square root, so the source of our issue resides in the realm of the Emperor. Perhaps we started off with good intentions and guidelines, but they lacked support and longevity. The foundation failed and everything came tumbling down.

Possible equations: $1 + 15$, $2 + 14$, $3 + 13$, $4 + 12$, $5 + 11$, $6 + 10$, $7 + 9$, 8×2, 4×4

7 + 9 = 16: Chariot: Forward Motion (7) + Hermit: Introspection (9) = The Tower (16)

We've lost sight of our goal. Maybe we were looking at the map instead of where we were going and we crashed. If we can figure out what distracted us, we can regain momentum and rebuild.

8 × 2 = 16: Strength: Mind, Body, Spirit (8) + High Priestess: Communication & Exploring the Mystery (2) = The Tower (16)

The foundation could not hold the structure we built on top of it. Maybe it was once good and solid, but that has changed. Now we can diagnose what went wrong, acknowledge that mistakes were made, clear away the mess, and actively focus on rebuilding.

Inner Math:

(1 + 6 = 7, Chariot)—To navigate through to the other side wiser and more focused

(1 × 6 = 6, Lovers)—Remember what moves us, our key values to rebuild upon

Exploring the Magic: People may be uncomfortable with the Death and Devil cards, but the real card that stresses out folks who are in the know is the Tower—and with good reason! The Tower tells us that the foundation we built our goals upon has cracked and the world seems to be tumbling down around us. It can signify divorce, loss of a job, natural and human-made disasters, and the breakdown of other kinds of relationships and securities—but it can also mean the destruction of institutions and ideas that we *thought* were helping us but were actually holding us back. Even though we may be incredibly stressed and thrown off by the incidents the Tower indicates, we will likely feel renewed and grounded once we get through the debris.

Both Kali Ma and Sekhmet are deities who have been in my personal practice since my days as a Witchlet. These fierce goddesses both have stories about destruction, chaos, and rebirth—about great battles fought and won and overcoming adversity. There is power to be found in the Tower. Nobody wants to go through these things, but I think it helps that the Tower reminds us we have been here before. The lightning, which was inevitable, has struck, illuminating the darkness in the process. We see by the light of the phoenix's embers that we can be reborn and soar once again. It's time to let things fall and clear the path for a new foundation.

The Star

The Number: 17

The Shape: Shooting star

Snapshot: A naked figure kneels at the edge of a pond, holding a vessel in each hand. One they pour into the water and the other onto the land. The sky behind them is filled with stars.

Musing: *Hope is on the horizon.*

Core Principles: Hope on the horizon, inspiration, future focus, illumination, give-and-take

Add It Up: Even though seventeen is an odd number, we would be wise not to mistake "uneven" for "unbalanced," as this card encourages us to stabilize ourselves. The thing about odd numbers is they actually make for stable bases when the ground is shaking. Yes, 4 makes a sturdy base, but cauldrons typically have 3 legs, which makes them less likely to spill when set on uneven ground. The Tower just made a whole lot of mess, and we, too, won't spill as much if we are a little uneven in this moment.

Possible equations: 1 + 16, 2 + 15, 3 + 14, 4 + 13, 5 + 12, 6 + 11, 7 + 10, 8 + 9

8 + 9 = 17: Strength: Mind, Body, Spirit (8) + Hermit: Introspection (9) = The Star (17)

We call upon our strengths to fortify us. We are the light in the darkness that will guide us forward.

7 + 10 = 17: Chariot: Forward Motion (7) + Wheel of Fortune: Change (10) = The Star (17)

There is a season for everything. The wheel continues to turn and we will navigate our way through the chaos into a new, brighter tomorrow.

Inner Math:

(1 + 7 = 8, Strength)—To find ourselves empowered, mind, body, and soul

(1 × 7 = 7, Chariot)—Keep your eyes on the prize, maintain forward momentum.

Exploring the Magic: The Star is a new day dawning. The number 17 brings a new spark of hope, blessings of illumination, the spirit of inspiration, and so many future possibilities.

As we navigate past the Tower, I am reminded of the expression "It is always darkest before the dawn." But also, the best way to view the splendor of the stars is on a dark night in an isolated place. But we are not alone in the dark. We are together, we are strong, and we are getting ready for our future.

When I look at the Star card, I am struck by two major visual elements. The first is that our figure is very active and also very naked. While Temperance stands fully robed, the Star is both vulnerable and free—and not afraid to get down to work. In being naked, we are reminded of the Lovers card (in pursuit of what moves our hearts) and the Devil card (letting go of that which does not serve us). The active work of the Star is taking care of the self (symbolized by the water poured into the pond) and taking care of others (the water poured onto the land). Both are done at the same time to achieve a sense of balance. It is also wise to note that the water poured onto the land drains back into the pond, which means the work we do for others in turn feeds and supports us.

The other major visual element of this card is the stars in the sky, all with 8 points. We have 1 major star surrounded by 7 smaller stars—8 stars total. This symbolism brings back the Strength card at number 8. When we address the needs of our mind, body, and spirit, we revel in strength and resilience. We are more prepared and ready for the work ahead. We just need to look for the right constellation to guide us.

Lastly, we often say the Star is a card of hope, the shooting star on the horizon that we make a wish upon. Hope is not whimsy or ungrounded idealism, but something that is hardy and enduring. Hope is power and fuel for the path ahead, creativity engaged and ready to process the possibilities. Hope is an opportunity not only to imagine what's possible but also to find our way to make the impossible possible. It is never wrong or shameful to have hope or to foster it—as long as we know we're preparing to do what we can to bring that hope into this reality.

The Moon

The Number: 18

The Shape: Moon phases (crescents and circles)

Snapshot: Dogs howl at a full moon that rises between two towers. Not far from them, a crustacean crawls out of the water.

Musing: *The unconscious rises to the surface.*

Core Principles: Call to introspection, lunar mysteries and powers, what lies below the surface

Add It Up: A lunar month is recognized as being 28 days—that's just 10 more than 18, summoning the Wheel of Fortune with its cycles. The number 28 divided by 3 gives us 9.3 repeating—hinting at the Empress (3) and the Hermit (9), which can correspond respectively to the waxing and waning states of the Moon as well. Plus there are 13 lunar months in a year, so Death is close by to help with transformation when we call upon the powers of the Moon.

Possible equations: $1 + 17$, $2 + 16$, $3 + 15$, $4 + 14$, $5 + 13$, $6 + 12$, $7 + 11$, $8 + 10$, 3×6, 9×2

3 × 6 = 18: Empress: Creativity & Choices (3) × The Lovers: What Moves Us (6) = The Moon (18)

The moon moves through three states: absolute (full or dark), waxing, and waning. In each phase, we must check in with our hearts to maintain our power.

9 × 2 = 18: Hermit: Introspection (9) × High Priestess: Communication & Exploring the Mystery (2) = The Moon (18)

The Moon asks us to look deeper within ourselves and face our unresolved fears and traumas. The High Priestess attends the rite to aid us. At the root of 9 is 3, the Empress, so she too—along with the Hermit—is here to support us. We just need to show up for ourselves.

Inner Math:

(1 + 8 = 9, Hermit)—To reach resolution with our past, oneness with our goal

(1 × 8 = 8, Strength)—Our strength comes from within, from challenging who we were to become a better, more whole version of ourselves.

Exploring the Magic: We have the Star to guide us in the dark, but it's the Moon that reflects the sun and lights the path before—and behind—us. At 18, the Moon is a call to introspection, to seek the great lunar mysteries, to consider the power of the tides to help us ebb and flow. The Moon holds power over liminal places and our subconscious and unconscious minds.

The Moon card feels a bit dangerous, with barking dogs and crawling crustaceans. That's because there's a warning here: Deal with the stuff you've been hiding below the surface and stuffing away in closets. The past is lurking and rising up via your dreams and other subtle signs around you. Pay attention and Witch up! Those dogs are your intuition telling you that you can't move forward without doing some emotional, mental, or spiritual housecleaning. And if you think you can ignore the howling of the dogs, you can bet that the lobster is coming in for a startling pinch of reality. Because as the song goes (in my head anyway), "In the Moon card, the wild Moon card, the lobster screams tonight."

The Sun

The Number: 19

The Shape: The sun or shield

Snapshot: A young child rides naked on a white horse while holding a red banner aloft. Behind them the sun shines fully and flowers are blooming.

Musing: *Success and good fortune shine upon you.*

Core Principles: Joy, happiness, success, recognition, celebration, family

Add It Up: At 19, we are almost at the end of our second cycle. The shape of the Sun or shield is reminiscent of the enneagon. We feel the many rays reaching out and touching all aspects of our lives.

Possible equations: 1 + 18, 2 + 17, 3 + 16, 4 + 15, 5 + 14, 6 + 13, 7 + 12, 8 + 11, 9 + 10

9 + 10 = 19: Hermit: Introspection (9) + Wheel of Fortune: Change (10) = The Sun (19)

Our time spent in contemplation and preparation has paid off. The care that we have taken pays us back tenfold with blessings and good fortune.

Inner Math:

($1 + 9 = 10$, Wheel of Fortune)—Our success shines brightly and brings happiness.

($1 \times 9 = 9$, Hermit)—Recognize that you deserve happiness and you can also be a beacon for others.

Bonus: If we break down 10 into its digit components, we have $1 + 0$: the Magician and the Fool. This pair, in the context of the Sun, says that wonder and wisdom can be a joyous combination.

Exploring the Magic: At 19, the Sun announces that this is a time for celebration. Acknowledge your success, rejoice, and be happy! This cycle is nearing completion and there's a sense of wholeness and contentment. You've made it past the dangers of the Moon (even the screaming lobster) and it's time to bask in the sunshine. The Sun can signify marriage, children, good health, prosperity, academic achievements, social recognition—whatever that big goal is that you've been working toward.

To keep the blessings of the Sun going, it is wise to share them. Don't hide them or be stingy, lest you lose them. If someone is jealous, that's on them, not you. Your path is forward. Soak up the sun and let it reflect on others without bias. Revel, rest, and enjoy.

Judgement

The Number: 20

The Shape: Asterisk

Snapshot: An angelic figure sounds a trumpet while ecstatic figures rise in praise out of their graves.

Musing: *To be judged is to be known and seen.*

Core Principles: The Wheel of Fortune come full circle, emergence, resolution, spiritual awakening

Add It Up: With 20, we've reached the end of our second cycle and are starting to move into the next one. The asterisk is the symbol for this card not because the shape works mathematically but because of what the asterisk symbolizes when it comes to computer programming. The asterisk can stand in for anything and point to other ideas. That feels spot-on for where we're at because what's next is undecided, although we may have an idea of where we want to go.

Possible equations: $1 + 19$, $2 + 18$, $3 + 17$, $4 + 16$, $5 + 15$, $6 + 14$, $7 + 13$, $8 + 12$, $9 + 11$, 10×2, 5×4

$4 \times 5 = 20$: Emperor: Foundation & Structure (4) × Hierophant: Spiritual Legacy (5) = Judgement (20)

Rebuilding or reevaluating our foundation while addressing what is spiritually important to us has led to greater understanding and resolution.

$10 \times 2 = 20$: Wheel of Fortune: Change (10) × High Priestess: Communication & Entering the Mystery (2) = Judgement (20)

Why not spin the wheel again? Are you feeling lucky? You should! You've gained perspective and you are in control of the situation. Be confident in making your next step.

Inner Math:

($2 + 0 = 2$, High Priestess)—Now we are the keepers of the temple; we know the mystery.

($2 \times 0 = 0$, Fool)—Look at how far we've come; don't forget to hold onto wonder.

Exploring the Magic: At 20, Judgement is the Wheel of Fortune doubled. It doesn't feel like the same wheel, but rather we have leveled up and are moving on to something greater or at least different. The appearance of this card may seem to reference eternal judgment, but we also know that the whole structure of the Tarot is based on cycles, wheels spiraling on top of each other. An end is just the start of another beginning. This card signals the end of one cycle, the resolution of whatever you've been working for. With $2 \times 0 = 0$, we're back with the Fool, but we've retained everything we learned along the way.

Also, regarding the idea of judgment—it's essentially an evaluation of how you've done, compared either to yourself or to others. You can be judged lacking, but you can also be judged worthy. You can be judged and lose, or you can be judged and win. And sometimes it's just about passing through, neither a win nor a loss on the table.

It's time to pack—remember the Fool's bindle? Hopefully you've upgraded to a carry-on that fits in the overhead bin. What will you take with you? What will you leave behind and lay to rest? Remember, "anything is possible" is on the menu.

The World

The Number: 21

The Shape: Ouroboros

Snapshot: A nearly naked figure dances in the sky, surrounded by a ring of laurel leaves.

Musing: *We have reached the end and the beginning.*

Core Principles: Completion, celebration, a new cycle begins with greater wisdom and understanding.

Add It Up: The number 21 is pretty magical, wrapping up the Major Arcana with the World. Thanks to my Great Uncle Joe, whenever I hear the number 21, I think of the card game blackjack. At one New Year's Eve party when I was still in single digits, he taught me how to play. That's probably another reason why I'm fascinated with numbers! To win at blackjack, you have to get as close to 21 without going over. Sometimes you can do it in just two cards (hitting 21 exactly) and other times you keep telling the dealer "hit me" to get another card, hopefully without going over. Well, you've done it—you've hit blackjack and the prize is you.

Possible equations: $1 + 20$, $2 + 19$, $3 + 18$, $4 + 17$, $5 + 16$, $6 + 15$, $7 + 14$, $8 + 13$, $9 + 12$, $10 + 11$, 7×3

$7 \times 3 = 21$: Chariot: Forward Motion (7) + Empress: Creativity & Choices (3) = The World (21)

You've done it! You studied the map, you kept on track, and you used the abundance and creativity of the Empress wisely. Excellent job! Congratulations!

Inner Math:

($2 + 1 = 3$, Empress)—As we begin a new cycle, we find ourselves renewed and at ease.

($2 \times 1 = 2$, Priestess)—Remember who you are and what you've overcome.

Exploring the Magic: At 21, we've reached the last card of the Major Arcana: the World. What's better than dancing in the sky partially naked? Knowing you've done a great job doing it! The World is your oyster in this moment. You can celebrate now that you have completed the work with tremendous success.

Our dancing figure is holding two wands, or perhaps they are batons. Their feet move toward the future, their torso faces the present, and their head faces the past. I like to interpret this as them passing the baton to their past self (or perhaps the next person entering the cycle) in recognition of their hard work. Maybe it's going to become the bindle for the next Fool or rest on the Magician's altar. The other wand or baton is the idea of what's next, being passed to the future self. Maybe it's being passed into the realm of the Minor Arcana. Either way, with torso forward, they celebrate this moment, right now, in the present, between the two. This is why the ouroboros makes an excellent symbol for this card. The cycle will continue on, being informed by the past as we set our sights on the future.

The cycle will continue on, as shall we as we explore the wonders and lessons the Minor Arcana cards have in store for us. I hope you have some room in your bag for a Wand, a Sword, a Cup, and a Pentacle!

CHAPTER 5

Minor Arcana—the Number Cards

The wonder of the little mysteries! The Minor Arcana cards are how the details of everyday life—from specific situations regarding work, health, family, and love life to the people involved and potential problems and repeated patterns—are expressed. The Major Arcana are like the chapter headings of a book or looking at whether you're eating breakfast, lunch, or dinner. The Minor Arcana are characters and plot points or the ingredients for what's on the menu.

We just learned 0 through 21 in the Major Arcana, which means we already have excellent insight into how numbers work in the Minor Arcana. We will refer back to the energy of the numbers from the Magician at 1 to the Wheel of Fortune at 10 when looking at the Aces through Tens. The court cards (Page, Knight, Queen, and King) are technically not numbered, so we will use a slightly different approach for those cards, as you will see. But having now been introduced to the flow of the numbers in the Major Arcana, you'll find that you're well on your way to understanding 40 of the Minor Arcana already!

It's Elemental, My Dear Reader

Before we dive into seeing how numbers work with the Minor Arcana, I want to talk about elemental associations—and my preference for what some practitioners view as a somewhat heretical approach to two of the suits.[21] This might be a revelatory game-changer for you, an affirmation of your own thoughts, or it might piss you off. Sorry/not sorry.

First, elemental associations are based on the idea that each of the suits of the Minor Arcana corresponds to one of the four classic elements: Air, Fire, Water, and Earth.[22] They are seen as being integral to life and are present all around us and even within us. Each element has certain characteristics and qualities that tend to be attributed to it. Each zodiac sign is connected to an element, which we look a little deeper into shortly.

If you're a magical practitioner, you may be wondering where Spirit is. Well, Spirit is present in the Major Arcana—and, I would argue, throughout all the cards, the reader, and the querent (if they are not one and the same).

Understanding these elemental associations can enhance your understanding of the cards and what you're looking at in a spread. At a glance, you can determine whether you're dealing with a lot of emotionally rooted issues or relationships, or perhaps it's important news about work and finances. You can also get some additional insight into how someone's sun sign may influence how they are best suited for what the cards are speaking to.

In many modern decks you will see the following associations:

Wands = Fire

Swords = Air

Cups = Water

Pentacles = Earth

These popular associations are believed to have come largely from certain orders of ceremonial magic—particularly the Hermetic Order of the Golden Dawn, of which RWS Tarot creators Arthur Edward Waite and Pamela Colman Smith were members. There has been a lot of discussion over the years about which tool/elemental associations are given to the

21. It may not be actual heresy, but if you ask the internet about this topic, pot holders might be needed to handle some of the opinions and how they're served.

22. There are traditions and cultures that recognize more elements than Earth, Air, Fire, and Water, as well as some that identify fewer—but the majority of magical practices often include these four in some way.

public and entry-level folks and which are given to those who become more advanced in that system.[23]

As a Witch, I tend to follow a different way of thinking when it comes to tools. I agree with two out of those four pairings: the Cups (Water) and the Pentacles (Earth). These associations are pretty obvious, in both a symbolic and a literal sense. Cups hold water and deal with the realm of emotions. Pentacles—also known as Coins or Discs—relate to the Earth-based concepts of wealth, health, and other physical concerns.

Now let's consider the last two tools: Swords and Wands. I tend to see Swords as Fire and Wands as Air. Swords are largely made of metal, which means they are forged in fire under great pressure. Once something has been exposed to fire, it is forever physically changed. Likewise, when you cut something with a sword or dagger, you are also permanently impacting the target. It can't go back to its original state. You can't uncut or unslice someone or something with a sword. One might be able to recover and heal or ask forgiveness for whatever action was taken, but the original action cannot be undone. To me, this is the quintessential essence of action. You make a choice that becomes an action and the situation is changed.

Wands are made of wood, which is also Earth if you think about it. Folks argue that you can set wands on fire, so it's natural for them to be associated with Fire. But we're not typically setting wands on fire; we're using them to direct energy, to stir, and to guide. A staff can be used to lean on and sticks can be used to draw lines in the sand. You can hit someone with a staff, but the damage is generally not as permanent as that inflicted by a sword.[24] A staff is also essentially the base of a broom—and brooms are very much tied into witchy folklore as something we take

23. If you search for "golden dawn elemental association tools switch," you will find many Reddit threads and numerous blogs pontificating about the reasoning and history. In fact, wherever you mix a group of occultists and booze, there's a good chance that someone is going to be talking about this very thing. And it's been going on for decades.

24. Please don't email me about martial arts and combat techniques. I know. You can also kill someone with a cup by poisoning them or if you drop a coin from a great height. By the way, I'm not endorsing violence. I'm just saying these things are possible. Remember, we're talking about symbols, ideas, and actions.

flight on (more Air!). Or, more mundanely, a staff or stang can provide support for your journey as you negotiate difficult terrain. We're really not using them for kindling, unless shit's gotten really bad. In some instances, you can even take a branch, place it in water, and grow a tree from it. The idea is that there's a lot of potential here, which is at the heart of Air. Air is all about ideas and possibilities, words and exchanges. Air is necessary for Fire to occur. Likewise, actions are often fueled first by ideas. We think, then we act. Even if instinct is involved, there's an idea or history behind the behavior.

But actions can also be fueled by emotions (Water) as well as instinct (Earth). Did I mention I'm an overthinker?

Even when I look at the original Rider-Waite-Smith deck, I don't see the Wands as being very fiery or the Swords as being very airy. In fact, when I look at the Wands, I get a sense of openness, light, bucolic landscapes, and open space. When I look at the Swords, the clouds read as smoke, the mountains feel volcanic, and the depictions feel heavy, closed-in, and permanent. Perhaps this was Pamela Colman Smith hinting at a deeper complexity in her illustrations per possibly Golden Dawn secrets. Yes, there are salamanders present in some of the Wand cards, and salamanders are traditionally seen as elemental beings of Fire. Yet there are birds in the Sword cards, not sylphs, and fish in the Cups, instead of undines. We don't see gnomes in the Pentacles; we see grapes as the popular motif. Rather than being representations of elementals, I think these symbols hint at relationships and influences. The salamander can regenerate parts of itself, just like an idea. But if we take the Fire aspect into consideration, it can be a reminder that the ideas we consider fuel the next step into action. Birds are symbolic of thoughts, but especially memories, so as we engage in action, we should remember the idea that got us here. Fish not only swim in water, but also live and breathe in it. Similarly, we must recognize where our emotions come from, immerse ourselves in them, and understand them—but we cannot live in water ourselves. We must come up for air. Grapes are a fruit of the earth but are only produced in the right conditions, and processing them takes time and investment—both thought and action. There are more layers of symbolism to be uncovered with the motifs we find in the Tarot, and no symbol exists in a vacuum. There's always more to it and how it relates to the whole of the story.

In the Tarot of Marseilles, we don't really see elemental representations at all. A lot of the earlier popular decks that were based on the RWS also tend to be pretty neutral. However, flipping through the Thoth deck, you'll see symbolism and colors that definitely read more fiery in appearance for the Wands suit. I have a theory that the Robin Wood Tarot, which became popular as a more colorful and Pagan-feeling deck soon after its release, combined inspirations from both the RWS and the Thoth. Then, after that deck was released, many more artists based their interpretations more on the Robin Wood than the original RWS.

Besides the correlations and uses that I feel are more potent for connecting Wands with Air/ideas and Swords with Fire/action, I find that the zodiac associations also ring very true. Aquarius, Gemini, and Libra are Air signs, so they correspond to Wands. Aries, Leo, and Sagittarius are Fire signs, so they are represented by Swords. Pisces, Cancer, and Scorpio are Water signs, so they align with Cups. That means the Earth signs of Taurus, Virgo, and Capricorn are Pentacles.

Again, it may be my bias of reading with this interpretation for over two decades, but I find that the personalities of the court cards, when aligned with my associations, fit better with what I know about those zodiac signs and how I've experienced them.

In the greater scheme of things, I think it's wise to recognize that all the elements not only are present in all the cards but are present in us as well. We don't call them into a magic circle because they weren't already present beforehand; we call them to make connections. So do allow some flexibility and room for crossover. The universe is messy, and by design, so are we.

Tempest's Elements and Suits Associations

Element	Suit	Associations
Air	Wands	ideas/breath/concepts
Fire	Swords	actions/change/effect
Water	Cups	emotions/relationships/memories
Earth	Pentacles	finances/money/physical concerns

Zodiac Interplay

Air	♒ ♊ ♎ Aquarius, Gemini, Libra
Fire	♈ ♌ ♐ Aries, Leo, Sagittarius
Water	♓ ♋ ♏ Pisces, Cancer, Scorpio
Earth	♉ ♍ ♑ Taurus, Virgo, Capricorn

Aces Through Tens

Now that we've covered the elemental associations, let's dive into the little mysteries! For the Aces through Tens, we'll look at the theme for each number and what lessons we might glean from that number's association with the correlating Major Arcana card, then I will do a quick breakdown of each suit. Now, there's so much more that every card can tell us, and what a card has to say will change depending on the deck, the spread, the reader, the querent, or the day! But there is a base type of expression that typically happens when the number interacts with the elemental energy of each suit.

My goal is to give you some ideas about how to interpret a card quickly using these guidelines. The more you sit with any card and consider it alongside others, the more information may come through. Sometimes a card will stand out to you as having a completely different meaning for one particular reading. You may find that the reason for this has to do with personal symbolism or some other message that is related to whoever is receiving the reading. There have been readings where I had an oddball feeling about a card, went with my gut in interpreting it, and discovered that the client connected immediately with the symbols or story received. They wouldn't have had that experience if I had gone with the traditional meaning for that card. Being a good reader isn't just knowing the cards well but also being open to being guided by your intuition when things don't match up neatly with the book interpretations.

You'll also notice that the higher the numbers go, the more work the cards may suggest to do. This is a natural progression as we go from the simplest form of each suit and work our way to its most complex or complete form. The higher we climb, the more responsibility we take on.

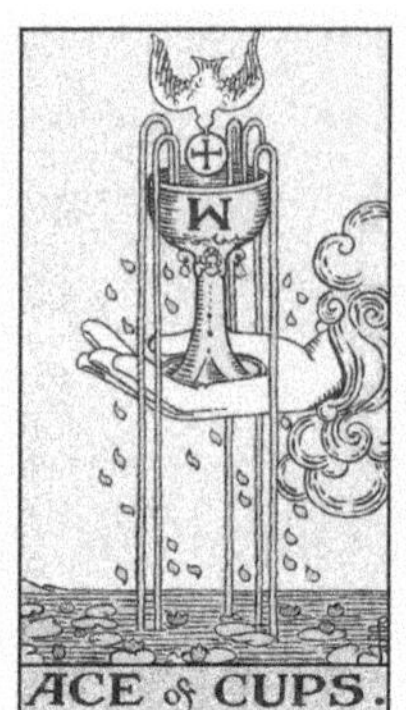

Aces

Themes: New start, focus

What the Magician Teaches Us About the Aces: The Magician has all the tools present and placed at the altar, ready to be used in order to understand and experience them. The Aces represent the core essence of each suit. They are the starting point for exploring the energy of a suit, ready to be engaged with. Aces can point to a singular focus or opportunity being presented.

Ace of Wands: A new idea to explore or engage with

Ace of Swords: A decisive action that sets things in motion

Ace of Cups: A new emotional opportunity that can be fulfilling and exciting

Ace of Pentacles: A boon, gift, or financial opportunity

Twos

Themes: Dualities and communication

What the High Priestess Teaches Us About Twos: Within dualities, we can have pillars of support or opposing forces. There's more than meets the eye here with the Twos: The unknown is at play and there's the potential for growth. We can find support or opposition, or perhaps a neutral space in between. The trick to navigating Twos is to overcome your fears, listen carefully, and seek clarity. Be willing to engage in a conversation and find out the real story.

Two of Wands: An exchange or sharing of ideas, comparing inner and outer visions, consulting for clarity

Two of Swords: Deception, uncertain or conflicting actions obscure the truth, exercise caution

Two of Cups: A meeting of the hearts, attraction, partnership, finding mirrored affinity and connection

Two of Pentacles: Weighing strengths and weaknesses, pros and cons, compromise, balancing opportunities, two sides of the same coin

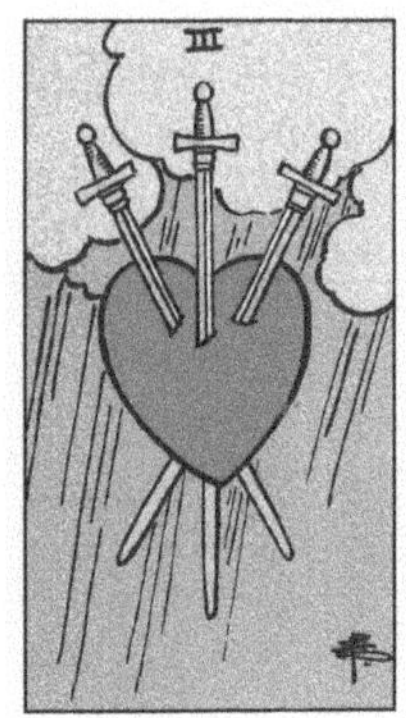

Threes

Themes: Choices, possibilities, development

What the Empress Teaches Us About Threes: The Empress is all about abundance, creativity, and the possibilities that come with having choices. So with the Threes, we are working with energy that can help create our future.

Three of Wands: Due diligence is needed to determine which idea is the best course of action to follow. Consider all the angles first so you can make an informed choice.

Three of Swords: An unexpected or temporary loss. How you react is crucial for overcoming this setback because you can either sink into it or clear a path forward.

Three of Cups: Celebration, communing, creativity thrives with sharing and embracing your emotions, a sense of fulfillment and promise for future developments.

Three of Pentacles: Make the choice to invest time and effort now. Hard work and a focus on details will pay off down the line.

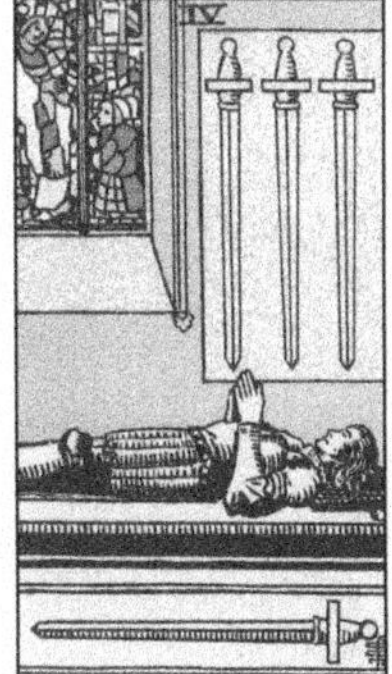

Fours

Themes: Foundations, balance, stability

What the Emperor Teaches Us About Fours: In order to prepare for the choices we made with the Threes, support is key. The Fours prompt us to consider balance, protocol, and what is fundamental for building the future we want.

Four of Wands: Honoring achievement. Successful unification of ideas creates a promising foundation for the future.

Four of Swords: Rest or inaction is the best course of action right now. It will stabilize and rebalance you.

Four of Cups: Avoid the "grass is greener" mentality—that is the dissatisfaction that comes from not appreciating what you have. This throws off your emotional well-being.

Four of Pentacles: It's natural to be conservative or controlling after achieving some success, but don't stifle prosperity with a fear of instability. Investment and support will give a bigger return if you loosen your hold.

Fives

Themes: Cycles; something has to change to break the pattern.

What the Hierophant Teaches Us About Fives: Occasionally we lose our way—often because we've become stuck in a rut of doing/saying/believing things that no longer suit us. Trauma can attach itself to traditions, dragging us down. Guidance and new insight can help us break free from damaging cycles.

Five of Wands: This is what I like to call the "someone is wrong on the internet" card—miscommunication feeds turmoil. You don't have to engage in competition or chaos in order to win.

Five of Swords: Too much ungrounded action or not enough meaningful action leads to dissatisfaction and waste. It's time to regroup and evaluate what has been working and what has not been successful. This will help you move forward with a better course of action.

Five of Cups: Unrequited love and/or irresponsible longing leads to depression and disillusionment. You're looking in the wrong place for love or fulfillment. Recenter yourself and focus on healing.

Five of Pentacles: Self-reliance is generally a good thing, but trying to do everything on your own leads to exhaustion, ruin, and loss. Accept help.

Sixes

Themes: Movement, reunions, harmony, blessings, journeys of the heart, body, and mind

What the Lovers Teach Us About Sixes: What moves us? What sets our hearts in motion? We are beginning to see and experience the fruits of our earlier choices in real time. We are in the flow and feeling it!

Six of Wands: On track for success, acknowledgment, harmony, community encouragement

Six of Swords: Indicates a departure into new territory, physical travel, exploration

Six of Cups: A journey to (or from) the past, happy reminiscing and reunions, family traditions that bring joy

Six of Pentacles: Upward mobility, sharing the wealth, investing wisely in the future, a sense of teamwork and accomplishment

Sevens

Themes: Pursuit, momentum, negotiating balance and control

What the Chariot Teaches Us About Sevens: With our hearts aligned, we're in motion, but we must keep our eyes on the prize and our hands steady at the wheel to navigate the course. The Sevens often point to the obstacle in our path that needs to be resolved in order to maintain momentum. What are we pursuing?

Seven of Wands: The conflict we face here is internal or from unreliable sources. Refocus on your goal, clarify your concept.

Seven of Swords: Subterfuge, stealthy action, succeeding despite the odds being against you. You can take the easy way out or work smarter.

Seven of Cups: Fantasy, illusions, and grandiose dreams can distract us from what's really important and what's actually possible. Don't be led astray by empty promises.

Seven of Pentacles: Patience and persistence are virtues that will pay off. Don't lose focus, make small adjustments as necessary, you're on track.

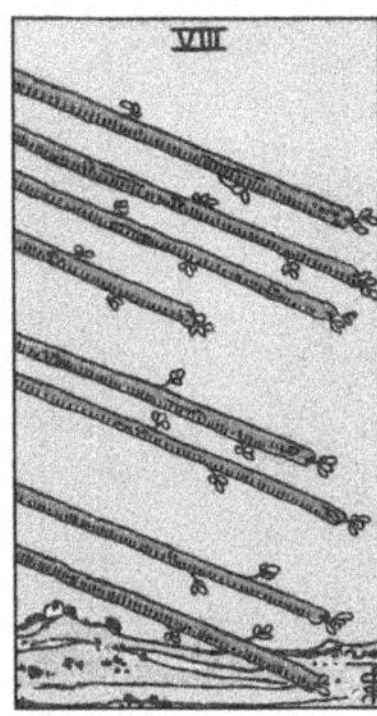

Eights

Themes: Capacity for strength, but what holds us back?

What Strength Teaches Us About Eights: Remember that 2 × 4 = 8: Strength can be the reliability of the Emperor doubled by the perception of the High Priestess, or the skill of the Magician combined with the speed of the Chariot puts us on track to be balanced. Eights want to be content and grooving along. They say we're almost there if we just make some slight adjustments to align and balance ourselves better.

Eight of Wands: Everything is aligning. There's consensus and motivation. The goal is clearly described. Just keep things on track.

Eight of Swords: Fear or indecision holds us back from moving forward and acting as we know we should. We must listen to our gut and free ourselves. No one else is going to save us here.

Eight of Cups: We are on the cusp of emotional fulfillment or satisfaction but feel we are undeserving or don't have what it takes. Release your fears and open your heart to what's possible.

Eight of Pentacles: Work well done, financial success, achieving mastery. Putting in the labor will pay off. Invest effort in the goal versus searching for accolades or recognition ahead of schedule.

Nines

Themes: Nearing completion, "almost there," evaluation

What the Hermit Teaches Us About Nines: The Hermit is all about introspection and illumination—and snacks. Our choices have grown (3 × 3), and now it's time to take a moment to examine their development, see what's working (or not), and refresh ourselves. We're almost there, but we may need to shift our perspective in order to fully succeed. This evaluation may change everything or affirm the track you're on.

Nine of Wands: Almost everything is in place and aligned, but it may be wise to reevaluate your premise and do some problem-solving before taking the next step.

Nine of Swords: Stress and anxiety may abound, but everything is already in motion. How do you deal with the inevitable outcome? You can either brace for impact or seek resolution and solace.

Nine of Cups: You may be getting what you want, but is it what you really *need* to be happy? Make sure your heart aligns with your goals and vice versa. Don't be afraid to be yourself.

Nine of Pentacles: The fruits of your labor are blooming all around you, but is it the right time to harvest? Trust your instincts and honor what you've accomplished.

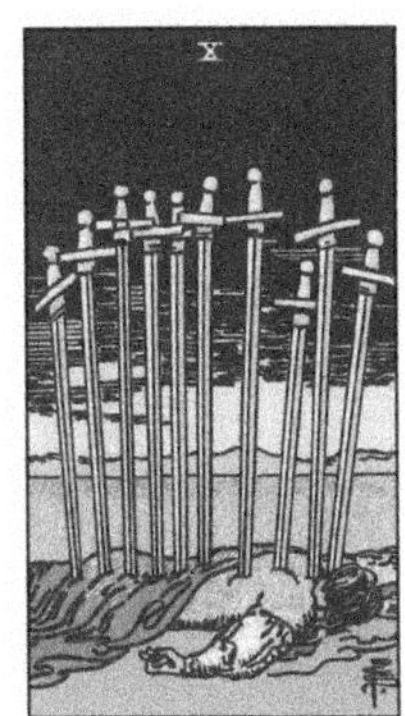

Tens

Themes: Completion, end of cycle, resolution

What the Wheel of Fortune Teaches Us About Tens: The Wheel has finished turning and we've arrived at the end of this cycle. Take some time to recognize the completion of this energy before moving on to the next cycle.

Ten of Wands: Your ideas have reached maturity and now it's time to carry them to the next phase: action.

Ten of Swords: You have reached the ultimate end. You can go no further; it is out of your hands.

Ten of Cups: Emotional fulfillment, joy, satisfaction. Love and happiness abound. Revel in this moment.

Ten of Pentacles: Success and fulfillment in the workplace, home security, wealth, financial stability.

The Court Cards

We've arrived at the "people cards." These cards can represent actual people or "faces," such as the querent, but also their family, love interests, friends, work acquaintances, etc. They can also represent situations and ideas.

This flexibility of being a person or something more archetypal can cause some apprehension when pulling these cards, but it doesn't have to be that way. I find that it becomes fairly obvious, depending on what situation I'm reading for and the variety of cards that show up in the spread and where. For example, if the querent is asking about their relationship with their parent, there are likely going to be court cards that represent the querent, the parent, and possibly any other influential people in the relationship. If a reading is more about personal growth and emotional development, multiple court cards can represent different aspects of the querent as they work through their issues. We will look more at how to interpret cards in spreads in chapter 7.

Before we dive into the specific court cards themselves, let's take into consideration a few things that will help us better understand what they represent.

Courting the Numbers

The court cards are not technically numbered, so what do we do here? Well, there are several concepts to consider. The first is that there is a progression or hierarchy to these cards, even if they're not numbered. First there are the Pages, followed by the Knights, next the Queens, and finally the Kings. Using this model, we can assign the following numbers to these cards:

1. Pages are young initiates learning their jobs and gaining experience. (1—The Magician)
2. Knights go on quests and great journeys. They must overcome their fears as well as respond to the call of duty. (2—The Priestess)

3. Queens are advisors and supporters and often symbolize the pinnacle of beauty, fertility, and artistry of their kingdoms. (3—The Empress)
4. Kings are the sovereign rulers, historically connected to the health and well-being of their countries. They govern to build, protect, and create prosperity in their kingdoms. (4—The Emperor)

These correspondences for the court cards make a lot of sense in relation to the Major Arcana when aligning their meanings. But what if, instead of starting back at 1, the court cards continued after 10? Then we would also see the following Major Arcana associations:

Pages—Justice (11)

Knights—Hanged One (12)

Queens—Death (13)

Kings—Temperance (14)

This set of correlations presents an interesting insight where the number cards here become specific challenges for each court card. For the Page, Justice represents seeking an education that will hopefully lead to a balanced and wise mind. How will they engage in the process and grow? The Hanged One paired with the Knight delves into the roles of service, ideas of sacrifice, and the quest for spiritual wisdom. What does the Knight seek to obtain and what are they willing to do to achieve it? Associating Death with the Queen takes on the challenge of renewal and transformation after destruction—birthing new ideas. When the Queen advises, who does the advice serve? And, if followed, does it create or destroy? For the King, Temperance points to self-control, dedication, and managing others fairly—resisting the temptation of absolute power leading to corruption. Can the King truly lead by example or is power being abused?

I think both pairings of associations are insightful in their own way. The first set (1–4) is beneficial for short readings or one-offs. The second set (11–14) comes in handy when you have time for a longer, more extensive reading or the querent is a repeat customer seeking deeper guidance. (And yeah, that querent can also be yourself!)

Age and Gender Expression

But *who* are these people represented by the court cards? What if the cards don't reflect the gender or age of the person being read for?

Even if the Tarot deck you're working with is very traditional in gender presentation, I invite you to think outside the binary. The court cards don't have to be cardboard examples of heteronormative relationships or traditional gender roles. I believe this is a feature, not a flaw.

Long before I came to understand terms like genderqueer and nonbinary, I was reading for folks who clearly aligned with the *personalities and qualities* of the court cards, even if their gender presentation didn't match up. I'm not saying that the querent was nonconforming, but rather that the cards representing them or the people in their lives absolutely were. Nor was I using a progressive deck—this was the late '90s and early 2000s, and remember, my main deck was Legend: The Arthurian Tarot. This deck is not exactly a shining example of queerness, at least when it comes to presentation and gender roles. My point is that you can be reading for anyone with any deck and the court cards may point more to personality and other characteristics versus aligning by gender alone. The best course of action is to trust your gut for each reading. You will also find that as you build up a relationship with a deck, you will have a feeling when there's more than meets the eye with the cards.

Some people get really cranky when you suggest thinking more creatively and inclusively with the court cards. Maybe for them it's more about the discomfort of not being able to take cards at their most obvious face value—which may say something about how they interact with people in general, so that's a whole ball of wax and red flags. But does it really make sense to automatically read the Queen of Cups as meaning that "a beautiful, fair woman with light hair and eyes who is dreamy and very emotional is coming into your life" if you're not going to also read the 5 of Wands as "four white dudes with big sticks are going to try and beat you up"? Sometimes the cards *are* very literal and things match up visually—but I think that's more the exception than the rule. Increasing your capacity for symbolism can enhance your intuition and understanding. It also doesn't hurt to be a more considerate, inclusive reader either.

Many modern decks incorporate gender-neutral language into their descriptions of the cards. I've included a few examples of each in the descriptions of the court cards for your consideration, as well as some other popular names for these cards. I think some of these titles help us see beyond gender and dig deeper into the hearts and minds of the people. More broadly, updating the language can help make the cards more relatable to more people than the classic terms do. This attitude in turn helps to create more meaningful, effective readings for a wider range of people.

Determining age in the court cards is another attribute that can be more symbolic than literal. A Page, for example, could be a child, a younger peer, or an emotionally immature person, or it could represent the querent's inner child. A Queen could be the querent, their partner, a boss, or a parent. The key is looking to see what role that card seems to be playing in the spread. It's also important to take the querent's age into consideration and how that may affect their perspective when interpreting court cards.

When you recognize that the court cards are just as symbolic as the rest of the deck, I think reading with them becomes easier. The next time you pull ten cards and six of them are court cards, you're not going to be caught up in, "Who the heck are all these people?" Instead, you'll see them as part of the pattern, motifs to be recognized with something to say.

Now, with the context of numbers and deeper symbolism, let us examine what the court cards may want to tell you.

PAGE of WANDS.

PAGE of SWORDS.

PAGE of CUPS.

PAGE of PENTACLES

Pages

Alternative Names: Messenger, Prince/Princess, Youth, Child, Student

Themes: Messengers, younger folks, or those less experienced bringing insight

Number Alignment: 1—The Magician, 11—Justice, Aces

Who Are They?: A page traditionally is a young person whose job involves running errands, delivering messages, and providing general assistance. They are learning how things work and may eventually take over the roles they assist with, so they are basically an apprentice. In the Tarot, they play the symbolic role of a message being delivered, or they can represent a young person, such as a child, or someone who is inexperienced or new to a situation.

Page of Wands: Bringer of ideas, full of energy and enthusiasm, talkative and intelligent. Air sign (Gemini, Libra, Aquarius).

Page of Swords: Bringer of secrets, often subtle and sly, restless, action-oriented. Fire sign (Aries, Leo, Sagittarius).

Page of Cups: The dreamer, prone to being very emotional, dramatic and dynamic (think theater kid). Water sign (Cancer, Scorpio, Pisces).

Page of Pentacles: A good helper who is steadfast, supportive, loyal, and determined. Earth sign (Taurus, Virgo, Capricorn).

KNIGHT of WANDS.

KNIGHT of SWORDS.

KNIGHT of CUPS

KNIGHT of PENTACLES.

Knights

Alternative Names: Champion, Journey, Adventurer, Traveler, Seeker

Themes: Journeys, quests, progression, maturing people

Number Alignment: 2—High Priestess, 12—Hanged One, Twos

Who Are They?: In history and lore, knights were elite soldiers who pledged allegiance to their rulers and were sworn to protect the land and its people in peace and war, all while maintaining a code of chivalry. The thing is, most of the time when you read about knights in stories, they're off on a quest or looking to take part in one. They're always on the move. Also, all our Knights are pictured on horseback, which not only is indicative of travel but represents duality as well. Horses have a mind of their own, so we have a balance between the will of the Knight and that of the horse carrying them. The horse can symbolize obligation, honor, expectations, and the pace at which the journey progresses. Knights can represent a metaphorical journey, but also a physical one. Knights can also indicate a maturing person, such as a teenager or someone finding out what it means to be an adult (at any age).

Knight of Wands: Thoughtful, courageous, intellectual, past-oriented. Air sign (Gemini, Libra, Aquarius).

Knight of Swords: Headstrong, in-the-moment, determined, acts first and asks questions (or for forgiveness) later. Fire sign (Aries, Leo, Sagittarius).

Knight of Cups: Romantic, future-oriented, driven by dreams, creative and playful. Water sign (Cancer, Scorpio, Pisces).

Knight of Pentacles: Financially or physically motivated, steadfast, future-oriented but not in a rush to get there. Earth sign (Taurus, Virgo, Capricorn).

Queens

Alternative Names: Counselor, Advisor, Artist, Visionary, Oracle

Themes: Supporting, directing, or advising role of the suit's energy

Number Alignment: 3—Empress, 13—Death, Threes

Who Are They?: Traditionally, the job of a queen (when ruling alongside a king) is to be a visual representation of their country, to provide support in governing, and to perform ceremonial duties. Metaphysically, a queen is a mystical embodiment of a country, its zeitgeist for that period of time. In the Tarot, Queens perform a similar role in representing the essence of their suit. In personality and presentation, they can embody the best, worst, or most stereotypical traits associated with their suit. A Queen can represent the querent or a partner, parent, sibling, peer, leader, or manager. Queens can help guide our choices within their realm of specialty.

Queen of Wands: Inspiring, capable, future-oriented, independent. Air sign (Gemini, Libra, Aquarius).

Queen of Swords: Well-informed, decisive, commands respect, sets hard boundaries. Fire sign (Aries, Leo, Sagittarius).

Queen of Cups: Empathetic, nurturing, past-oriented, whimsical, introspective. Water sign (Cancer, Scorpio, Pisces).

Queen of Pentacles: Detail-oriented, reliable, practical, conservative, aesthetically focused. Earth sign (Taurus, Virgo, Capricorn).

KING of WANDS

KING of SWORDS.

KING of CUPS.

KING of PENTACLES.

Kings

Alternative Names: Regent, Sovereign, Ruler, Architect, Elder

Themes: Authority, guiding or ruling energy of the suit's energy

Number Alignment: 4—Emperor, 14—Temperance, Fours

Who Are They?: The classic interpretation of a king is someone who is the figurehead or supreme ruler of their land. But true kings are in a position of power *with* the land, not *over* the land. To thrive, the country must be supported, protected, and structured for mutual prosperity. A king doesn't act alone, but with guidance from a council of advisors or parliament. The Kings in the Tarot become the consensus of their suits, for better or worse, depending on how they managed through their own journeys. A King can represent the querent or a partner, parent, peer, sibling, leader, or elder.

King of Wands: Charismatic, inspiring, sometimes unconventional. The ultimate idea person; generates and delegates versus delivers. Future focus. Air sign (Gemini, Libra, Aquarius).

King of Swords: Strong, persuasive, determined, all about getting things done. It may not be the right way, but it'll get done—right now. Fire sign (Aries, Leo, Sagittarius).

King of Cups: Sensitive, calm, enchanting, likes to reminisce. Goal-oriented but also prone to obsession. Water sign (Cancer, Scorpio, Pisces).

King of Pentacles: All the trappings of worldly success—family, friends, finances. Vibrant and sensual but can get too focused on reputation and appearances. Earth sign (Taurus, Virgo, Capricorn).

This completes our exploration of both the Major and the Minor Arcana. I would like to remind you that the interpretations included here are a baseline for you to build on. As you develop a relationship with your deck and do more readings, you will uncover a lot more that is particularly relevant to you and unique to your deck. That's definitely something you can count on.

CHAPTER 6
Holding All the Cards

All right, now that you are familiar with the Major and Minor Arcana and what they can mean, the next step, naturally, is to start using the cards for readings, right?

But before we jump into the magic of spreads and reading the cards, let's cover some technical things about the cards that a lot of folks tend not to consider. This includes how to prepare yourself for a reading, how to physically work with the cards, the issue of OPE (other people's energy), and creating a mobile setup.

Breathe by Three

Before you begin to shuffle and pull your cards, I recommend taking a breath to focus yourself and enter a receptive and creative state for both your mind and your body. I have a particular exercise that I use in my practice that I simply call the "Three Breaths." I use this exercise whenever I'm about to do divination, perform dance, lead a ritual, teach a workshop, or engage in any other activity that may require significant focus. When I can, I do this exercise using the whole of my body to conduct the air in and out, meaning my arms and legs are involved in the process. But you can also do this exercise from a seated position, without needing to move your arms or legs. The breaths are the most important part.

Three Breaths Exercise with Your Whole Body

1. To start, stand with your legs a little wider than shoulder width apart, with a bit of squishy bend in your knees, and have your arms loosely crossed in front of your belly/diaphragm.

2. As you first take a deep breath in, lower your center of gravity slightly by bending your knees. As you finish drawing the breath in, uncross and extend your arms outward in a welcoming position while straightening your knees slightly.
3. Hold the breath for three seconds, then slowly release, relaxing your arms down and bringing them back to center.
4. Repeat the whole movement again, this time holding your breath for six seconds, then release.
5. Lastly, follow the process one more time, holding for nine seconds, then release the breath.

Three Breaths Exercise from a Seated Position

1. To start, adjust your posture in your chair so you're sitting tall, with your back straight, chest and chin lifted. Have your feet in contact with the ground.
2. Take a deep breath in, focusing on pulling the breath into your belly/diaphragm. Hold the breath for three seconds, then slowly release.
3. With the second breath, focus on breathing into your chest (heart and lungs). Hold your breath for six seconds and then release.
4. On the third breath, focus on the breath entering your head (nasal passages). Hold for nine seconds, then release the breath.

After doing the exercise, whether standing or seated, you should feel calm, collected, and ready to accomplish the task at hand.

Taroruffle Shuffle

There are so many ways to shuffle and deal out the cards. I am going to share with you how I do it and why. See what works best for you.

When considering a question, whether for myself or for someone else, I shuffle the cards using a variation of the overhand shuffle. For this shuffle, you have a "holding" hand that maintains and secures the larger pile of cards and a "moving" hand that distributes smaller piles of cards back into the main chunk of cards. I hold the cards in my left (less dominant) hand and move the cards with my right (more dominant) hand. Take a section of the deck from your holding hand and then, with your moving hand, relocate that separated group back into the deck by placing it either on top, slipped into the middle, or at the back of the deck. This keeps the cards all facing the same direction and cuts down on wear and tear of the cards. I find the motion very meditative, and I move enough sections in large and small quantities that the cards do get mixed up fairly well. I alternate between top, middle, and back without consciously thinking about how I'm moving the cards.

If I'm reading for someone else, I take this time to ask them what they're looking to find out about (whether they have a specific question or area of interest or want a general reading) and what their zodiac sign is. It also gives me time to assess their energy and tap into it. Periodically as I shuffle the cards, I set them on their short edge to see if they "stick" together. This technique is something I've been intuitively doing for decades. Basically, if the cards stay in a solid pile, it's time to start the reading. If they split or fall apart, more shuffling is required.

Some folks don't feel like the cards get shuffled enough using the overhand method, but with my variation, where I place the cards in different spots and amounts throughout the process, they do get fairly well mixed. I also both count and time my shuffles for a typical reading. In about 50 to 60 seconds, I can shuffle the cards 40 to 50 times on average. It usually takes that long to get acquainted with a client and get them comfortable.

A riffle shuffle is where you split the deck into two piles and merge them together at the short end of the cards, interweaving them together. I like to think of it as a casino shuffle, as you often see flashy variations with playing cards. The riffle shuffle does a fairly good job of randomizing the cards over a few passes, but it also changes the direction of the cards, adding reversals to the mix. This may not bother you if you actively read reversals or have good wrist action where you rotate a reversed card as it comes up. What I like about the overhand shuffle keeping things in upright order is that if a card still manages to come up reversed or flies out of the deck, I see it as a sign to pay extra close attention to that card.

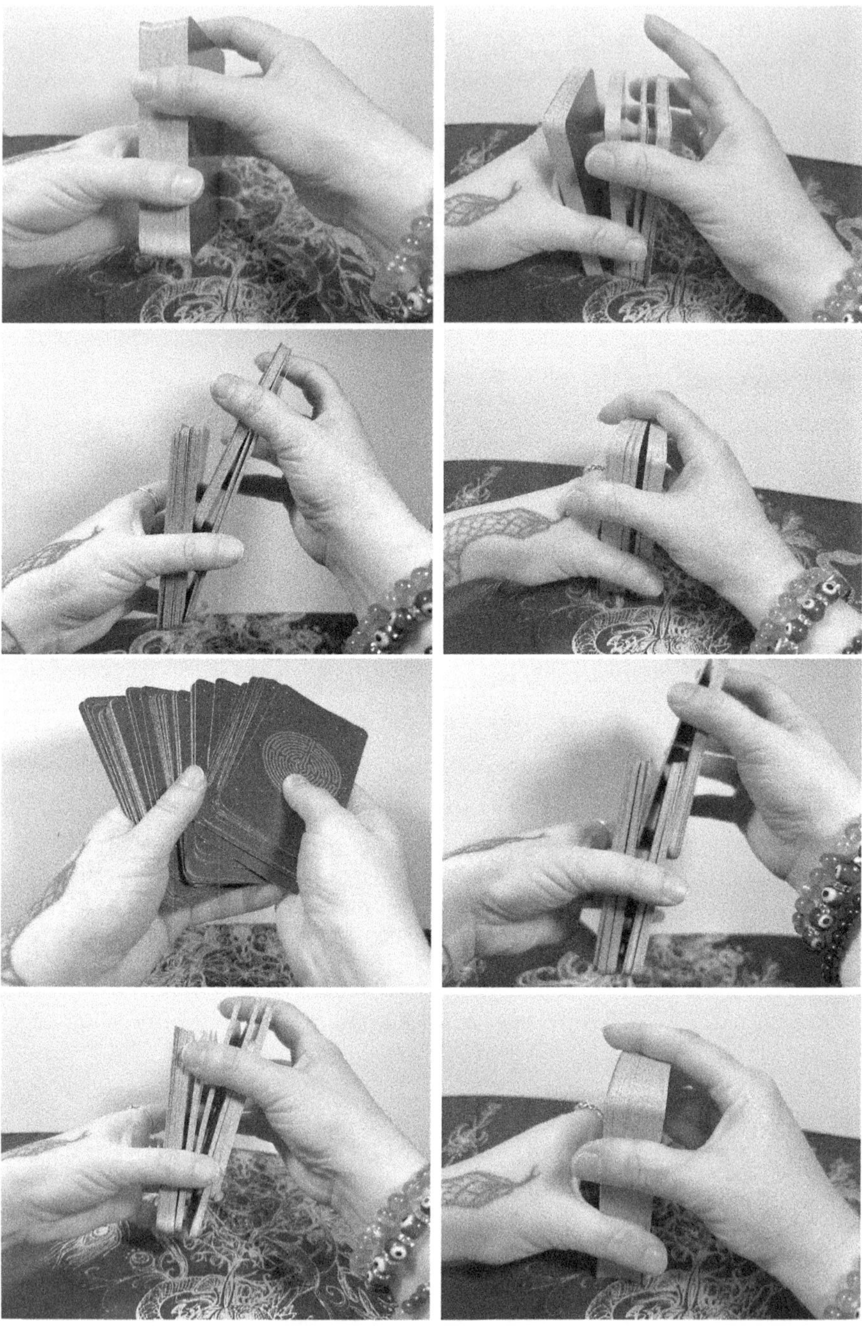

Tempest Demonstrates Their Version of the Overhand Shuffle

Another thing to consider is that playing cards are generally much shorter than Tarot cards, so the bend and friction on playing cards caused by the riffle isn't as stressful. Also, casinos change out decks frequently to keep them fresh, so there's damage but you're just not seeing it. With Tarot cards being longer in length than playing cards, there's more of a bend, and since the cards are more image-heavy, the damage appears more quickly. This may not be a big deal if you're just reading for yourself, but if you want to read on a professional level, you'll want to think about which deck you're using, how long it will stay nice, and if you're going to be able to affordably replace it. Basically, you don't want to be using a fancy limited-edition boutique deck constantly. It's better to find a mass-produced deck that you enjoy for this kind of work. There are popular decks that have been in print for decades that you may want to consider instead.

What If a Card Goes Flying?

Inevitably, at some point when you're preparing to do a reading, a card will fly out on its own. I like to make note of what that card is, discreetly tuck it back into the deck, and then shuffle some more. Sometimes that flying card is an important message to consider. Chances are it will show up in the reading as well.

If it's consistently the same card over and over again, then either you really need to pay attention to what the card is saying, especially if you're divining the same situation or question, or perhaps the card has some sort of physical issue causing it to stick or break away, so it may be time for a fresh deck. Not every movement is spirit-based. Sometimes it's just physics.

Touchy or No Touchy?

Some readers have the querent split the deck or shuffle the cards. This is a nice way to get them involved on another level besides asking a question. Some readers say it helps the cards "absorb" the energy of the querent. But that also means you're dealing with both the physical and the metaphysical residue of whoever is holding your cards, in which case you may need to consider doing a physical cleaning as well as a spiritual cleansing of your deck. The latter is fairly easy to do, but it's not so easy to clean paper without compromising its integrity. It can also be difficult to get folks to wash their hands before handling your cards, though you could provide hand sanitizer at your reading station, which can help somewhat. I've included some cleansing suggestions in the next section.

I'm one of those ~~assholes~~ readers who doesn't like people touching my cards, and I've always been this way. If you ever do readings at street festivals, bachelor/ette parties, or nightclubs, you just never know who's going to be handling your cards and how clean their hands are. Considering what the COVID-19 pandemic taught us, I'm even more inclined to keep my cards to myself. I find that as I shuffle the cards, if I keep the person engaged and a bit mesmerized by the motion of what my hands are doing, they are sufficiently content and relaxed.

Cleansing the Cards

Here are some suggestions for cleansing your deck and related tools and keeping everything in good working order metaphysically. Some of these techniques you may find helpful to do before or after every reading. Other suggestions you may wish to do as needed or as part of a monthly lunar ritual.

Movement-Based Cleansing: Tap and shuffle your cards. After I do a reading, I return all the cards to the pile, do another couple of quick shuffles, then gently tap them a couple of times on the table. It's a simple yet effective way to "clear" the cards and put them away—or prepare them for a different question. This tap is easy to do every time you read.

Smoke Cleansing: Many practitioners like to use some form of smoke cleansing to bless or reset their tools. Smoke combines the elements of Air, Fire, and Earth. It also engages the olfactory system, which is deeply tied to memory and the unconscious. You can perform smoke cleansing by burning a bundle of dried herbs or using incense. Choose herbs or incense blends that make sense with your practice and intention. You can make your own or purchase them. Light your bundle or incense in a safe container (such as a shell, dish, or bowl), then gently blow out the fire. As the smoke rises, wave your deck and other tools through it at least three times. As smoke (and stray sparks) can cause damage to paper, I recommend wrapping your deck first in fabric to protect it.

You can use premade incense or create your own blend or bundle. Look to see what's already growing nearby, as there's a wide variety of herbs you can use for cleansing.

If you plan on burning an herb bundle, set it in a firesafe dish or bowl to smoke. That way your hands can securely hold the wrapped deck and wave it through the smoke.

Tip: Don't burn your herbs or incense under a smoke alarm. An even better solution is to do this outside.

Cleansing with Smoke

Infused Spray Cleansing: If you can't use smoke because of allergies, smoke sensitivity, or other safety reasons, you could use an infused spray. If you're especially sensitive to scent (or are working with people who are), your infused spray can simply be blessed water, be it moon water, sacred spring water, sea salt–infused water, or olive oil–infused water. You can make (or buy) tinctures with your favorite herbs or oils mixed in as well. A lot of witchy shops sell their own brands of cleansing sprays, and there's also Florida water. Now, just as smoke isn't ideal for paper, neither is water, obviously, so don't spray it directly on your deck! You can, however, spray the area you're working on or spray the deck when it's safely wrapped in a cloth, bag, or box.

Crystals: Some readers use crystals for cleansing, protection, and amplification of psychic abilities. Others use them simply as beautiful decoration for the setup. And probably even more people work with crystals for their aesthetic and magical properties. The rockhound in me absolutely loves crystals, shells, and fossils from a geological perspective, and the artist in me is absolutely fascinated by their aesthetics. But in my personal practice, I don't actively use crystals from an energetic standpoint for specific properties and goals—except for one instance, and that's hematite. I no longer remember exactly where I acquired this little sphere of hematite, but it's been with me for most of my reading career. It's perfectly smooth and about the size of a golf ball. It fits perfectly in the palm of my hand. When I was a teenager, someone told me that hematite repels negativity and has grounding properties. I still make that connection in my brain, but more importantly, it's soothing to hold, it's beautiful to look at, and it can cause some damage if I need to throw it at someone or something quickly. It's also super easy to clean. So if this little sphere is doing double duty by being grounding and repelling negativity, that's absolute bonus points.

If you already use crystals in your practice, then by all means do combine them with your Tarot work. But recognize that if you're going to be working with the public and you place them in your setup, people might be handling them. If you don't use crystals but would like to know more, check to see who around you offers ethically sourced crystals and see what you're drawn to naturally, or discover what's hanging out in your own backyard. Here in New England, I can find several varieties of quartz just by hiking in the woods or going to the beach.

Remember, you don't have to use all these cleansing techniques every time you do a reading. If you are not sure what approach to use or are uncertain of what may work best for you, I suggest trying one technique at a time. See how the technique feels and if it aligns with your beliefs and magical practice. If you're still developing on that level as well, experiment! Take notes on which techniques you do and how and when you did them, plus any noticeable results. After a short time, you may start to notice a pattern of what works best for you.

A Mobile Altar

Another way to maintain your energy while at the same time creating a beautiful setup is to make a mobile altar. What is a mobile altar? It's a setup that includes several of the items we just discussed for cleansing and other items that have meaning for you. It also creates a mood or aesthetic that can add to the reading experience.

When I used to read professionally full-time, I had a whole kit that I brought with me to set up in the reading room. The kit was comprised of a beautiful ornate wooden box with a handle and lock, a bit bigger than a classic lunch box but smaller than a toolbox. Inside it held my go-to decks, a chime candle and holder, a large reading cloth for the table, some crystals, and other special small items for cleansing and protection. At the beginning of each shift, I would set up my mini altar on the reading table (or on a nearby shelf if there wasn't room) and consciously create sacred space. At the end I would break everything down and do a quick cleansing.

I don't have that box or ready setup anymore, but if I do happen to plan on giving some readings, my go-to deck is already wrapped in its own cloth in a zipper pouch with its own talisman. Nearby in my ritual cabinet I can select one of my larger table coverings and grab incense or a candle with appropriate holders, a lighter, and my trusty little sphere of hematite in its velvet drawstring pouch. All this fits easily and quickly into a tote bag and I'm ready to go.

When creating your mobile altar, think about the space you're going to be reading in (if you know ahead of time) and consider what would make it more comfortable for both you and your clients. Also, what is safe and appropriate for the space? If you plan on carrying oils or other liquids with you, keep them in their own bag to avoid accidental spillage. It's not a matter of *if* they will spill but *when*. Even if you're just creating a mobile altar to use for yourself, whether at home or when traveling, be mindful of what you're adding to your kit.

Suggested List for Your Tarot Setup:

- Table covering (or multiple ones if you need to provide a table cloth and also want a spread cloth)
- Cleansing materials (incense, bundle, spray)
- Crystals, shells, or other natural items
- Candle (live or electric)
- Protective items, elements, or mementos
- Miniature deity statues or other spiritual representations that are important to your practice
- Tip jar or plate

Your mobile altar should be something that's easy to bring with you, because hauling around a giant setup is a pain in the ass. You also don't want something that's too heavy or takes too long to set up and break down.

Now that you know how to best handle and care for your deck, it's time for the exciting part: using your deck! In the next chapter, we will explore spreads and how to read the cards using my techniques. It's shuffle time!

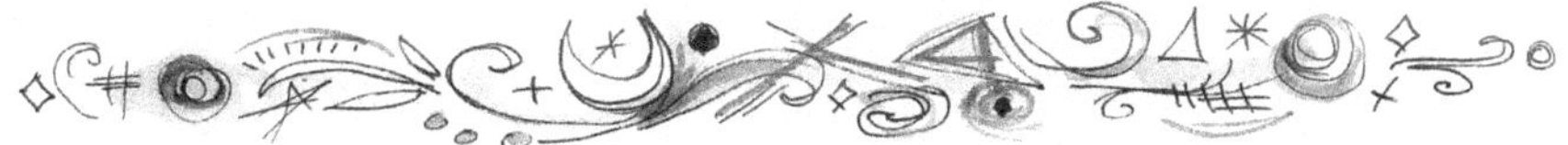

CHAPTER 7

Tarot Spreads—Mapping the Meaning

Now it's time to play with those numbers and shapes and see how everything comes together. This is where the magic happens!

In this chapter, we will explore how to use math in spreads for more effective reading. We will cover everything from what to look for in the cards to deciphering the patterns and symbolism of the cards. I'll share with you some of my favorite signature spreads and give you examples of how to read each one. Then I'll guide you through how to design spreads of your very own.

What Is a Tarot Spread?

A Tarot spread refers to the laying out and arrangement of cards in order to divine meaning. Pulling a single card isn't technically a spread, but once you start to involve multiple cards, relationships begin to form. Spreads are designed to assign meaning or purpose to a card depending on how and where the cards are placed. It is more effective to place cards with purpose instead of just throwing down a bunch of random cards.

While it may seem more "intuitive" to just keep pulling cards and laying them out, this is not a great way to get helpful answers or insight. Our minds like to reason their way in or out of anything, especially when the rules are downright squishy or nonexistent. You should technically be seeking clarity and revelation, not confirmation of bias. In order to avoid the latter as much as possible, you should decide what kind of spread you are doing *before* you start to lay the cards down.

Doing the Math: Assessing Spreads and Adding Up Meaning

Once you begin pulling the cards, there are some key ways that math comes into play. First there is the number of cards in the spread itself. As I just mentioned, you should know what spread you are going to do before you start laying out cards. The number of cards can be significant to the purpose of the spread, as we'll see later in this chapter.

Then there are the patterns and frequency of the numbers of the cards, besides where they are in the spread. Here are some questions you should ask yourself as you lay down the cards.

Which Major Arcana Cards Showed Up?

The first thing I do is play "spot the Major Arcana." This means noting how many of them showed up and where are they placed in relation to the spread's meaning, and noticing if their numbers correlate with any of the other cards. For example, if the Empress showed up, are there any other Threes? As the Major Arcana emphasize big themes and ideas, they're very influential cards for reading. Consider them the dominant flavor of a spread and don't ignore them.

How Many Cards of Each Suit Are Present?

Look to see how many Cups, Swords, Wands, or Pentacles are in the spread. This also helps us clue into the energy or major influences among the cards. If there is a large number of Cups, then there are a lot of feelings likely going on. If there are a lot of Wands but not many Swords or Pentacles, then a lot of thought and consideration is happening but perhaps not much action or physical results. Lots of Swords show that there's a lot of action going on, often with impact or consequences. A focus on Pentacles could indicate work and wealth situations, especially if the topic of a spread is finances—but as Pentacles relate to the physical realm, they can also refer to the querent's health. This is another reason that it's a good idea to be specific with your topics and questions.

Which Court Cards Are Present?

Who's hanging out in your spread? Which cards feel like they are specific people and which of them may refer more to situations? Are there a lot of a particular court card, such as Knights or Queens? Is there any sort of progression, such as all the court cards of a suit being present? Or is there a connection between the cards due to the layout? For example, perhaps each court card is represented but they are from different suits.

What Are the Numbers? Do Any Repeat?

Not only do numbers give us insight into the meaning and energy of each card, but when we look at a spread, there is also the collective energy of those numbers to consider. Look to see what numbers show up and if there are multiples of any of them. I'm technically already doing this when I survey the spread to see which Major and Minor Arcana are present. An example of a repeat would be if there's the 7 of Wands, the 7 of Cups, and the Chariot. Not only are we tapping into 7 to read into the individual meanings of these cards, but if 7 dominates the spread, that also indicates a theme for the querent—that they are actively in pursuit, but perhaps they still need to formulate a clearer idea of what they are actually in pursuit of. Similarly, if there are a lot of Threes, then we see the development of lots of choices to be made. If there are a lot of Fives showing up, then there is likely stagnation or unhelpful repetitive behavior. Additionally, if there is a clear progression of numbers or the numbers go up or down through the spread, then there is a sense of growth or change possible or happening. If we see a 4, 5, and 6 of a given suit, that indicates the querent is working through that challenge effectively.

What Relationships Do You Spot Between the Numbers and Placement of the Cards?

The next level is seeing deeper correlations between the cards by utilizing arithmetic operations: addition, subtraction, multiplication, and division. When we explored each of the cards in the previous chapters, I shared with you equations that can be found within each card—mostly addition, but some multiplication. Those examples are meant to give you ideas of how these cards can be combined for additional meaning or insight. When you are dealing with multiple cards versus a single pull, there's now an opportunity to notice how cards can be added up, multiplied, divided, or subtracted from.

For example, if a row in my spread is made up of the 9 of Cups, the 8 of Pentacles, and the Star (17), $8 + 9 = 17$. Therefore, those two Minor Arcana are each giving us a clue on how to work our way to the Star card—likely through healing yourself by addressing your own needs and keeping up the good work at your job, as it's leading you to bigger and better things down the line.

If my overall card is the Hermit (9) and my spread has a lot of Threes, we know that 3 is the square root of 9. The Hermit could be emphasizing the need to slow down, seek guidance, and really do some soul-searching before you start making choices.

You may be wondering how the various arithmetic operations differ. Well, they each have their own signature energy, although I'm disinclined to assign a moral value to them. They simply are how the universe moves—building up, breaking down, fast and slow, chaos and order. These processes are more for recognizing patterns and relationships between the cards due to their assigned numbers.

Addition: Focusing on the core components that build a number, a sense of steady increase

Subtraction: Reducing down to the simplest form or core elements, slow decrease

Multiplication: Magnifying the powers of the cards involved, amplified growth or increasing energy

Division: Getting down to the root, fast reduction or decreasing energy

Not every Tarot reading is going to have an obvious arithmetic operation you can spot, but since there are a lot of numbers in the Tarot, there's a good chance you'll recognize at least one if you're pulling multiple cards.

In the sample spreads I've included in the next sections, you'll see even more examples of how to notice relationships and play with the math. I promise that once you start making the connections, it will become easier and easier to spot them!

Does Anything Else Stand Out?

We've talked a lot about numbers and their energetic processes, as well as noting what suits are present, but one of the most wonderful things about the Tarot is that it can be a very visual experience. When you look at your spread, consider what visually stands out to you beyond the numbers and suits. Is there a dominant color or colors showing up? Are there lots of scenes showing conflict and chaos, or is the imagery calmer and more restful? Do you see lots of contrast or harmony? Perhaps the cards start out with a lot of conflict and become more settled and grounded as the spread continues. Do you see a lot of figures standing or lying down? Which way do the figures face? Are you suddenly spotting birds all over this spread even though it's not a deck inspired by birds? Obviously, the theme and aesthetic of a deck will determine much of what you see, but a well-designed deck will still have variety among the cards that creates different moods and feelings.

Allow yourself to play with what the artistic presentation of the deck is hinting at, especially if you have the time to dig a little deeper. I am an artist, so you might think the art is the first thing I look at in a reading, but typically I first consider the numbers and their patterns right off the top. *Then* I settle into the art for more revelation. The numbers give me a structure to work with for the reading. Essentially, using the math processes is like laying out the blueprint of a house and seeing how to navigate what's inside. They may even hint at what condition the house is in—a mess, under renovation, neatly ordered, or well maintained. The colors, symbols, and composition tell me what the lighting might be like in the house, how the rooms are decorated, and who lives in this house. The art can help fill out the structure in greater detail, adding another layer of life through thoughts, feelings, hopes, and memories. Remember, art is about human expression—and that's a big part of what the art is doing in your cards.

What About Reversals?

It's right about here in my workshops that someone asks, "But what about reversals? Do you read reversals?" I'm one of those people who doesn't read reversals—most of the time. Because of the way I shuffle and deal my cards, they all face the same way, upright. As I mentioned in the section on shuffling in chapter 6, other methods may lead to mixed-up cards. That may be a feature, not a flaw, if you prefer to have reversals. It really is a personal preference.

But if there are no reversals, does that mean I'm reading everything as all rosy? Nope! I'm reading the cards just like I read people: I look for clues. I listen to my intuition. No one's head is going to be on backward or upside down to tell me there's something amiss with them. The same can be true with the cards: When you tune into the rhythm of the Tarot, you can get a sense that there's more than meets the eye.

But occasionally the deck/the universe/some force out there *really* wants me to pay attention to a specific card. It either flies out of the deck or somehow manages to come up reversed despite the rest of the deck being upright. I take that as a sign to be extra careful about what that card can indicate in this particular reading.

How Does Timing Work with the Tarot?

Figuring out timing is probably one of the toughest things about pretty much any form of divination. Tarot is no exception. One way to narrow down timing is to focus your question with that information, so the spread's timeline is a week, month, year, etc. My threefold spreads (which we're about to explore) give a general sense of order and timing, but I'm rarely gleaning a specific date from the cards. Overall, I tend to get a sense of season for when something could happen or I'm perceiving some other information psychically where I may hear or see a month or date. So I'm not really getting that information from the cards specifically.

However, when it comes to considering the cards themselves, the Major Arcana tend to indicate big events or influences that absorb a significant amount of time. They're not single dates, but rather a stretch of weeks, months, or even years. The Minor Arcana, since they focus on smaller details and happenings, tend to have a shorter, more immediate focus. You could also pull a card with a specific timing question, like "When could this happen?" and use the number on the card to refer to a month, date, or amount of time—that is, if you've got a card with a number and not a court card.

The thing I often come back to though is this: Timing depends on the querent. Some people are proactive about making changes and other people simply aren't. If an event is dependent on the querent taking action, then that's the most important thing to relay about timing from the reading.

If someone wants the cards to tell them a specific date or time, that's not the Tarot's job.[25] Timing involves so many factors, so really the best answer you can give is an estimate based on what you see in the cards or on other clues you may be getting from your intuition. Or, if you're unsure, just say so. I have no problem telling someone that timing is hard to pin down and I can only provide an educated guess based on the information I have.

This information may all seem like a lot to think about, but the more you practice and play, the easier it becomes. You will start to notice the patterns as well as recognize arithmetic operations. You'll be able to take a quick glance at the cards and see what's happening on the surface level. Then you can peel back more layers of symbolism and meanings as you examine the cards individually and collectively. You can go as deeply into the cards as you'd like or as time allows. The more you look, the more you will notice!

Now it's time to play with the cards and see them in action. Let's examine some of my favorite go-to spreads and see how they work.

25. I suppose one could devise an oracle deck with dates specifically in mind: 12 cards for the months, 7 cards for the days of the week, 31 number cards, etc. (I honestly don't know if I love or hate this idea. I might have to try making one myself just to see!)

Simple Threefold Spread (The 4-Card Pull)

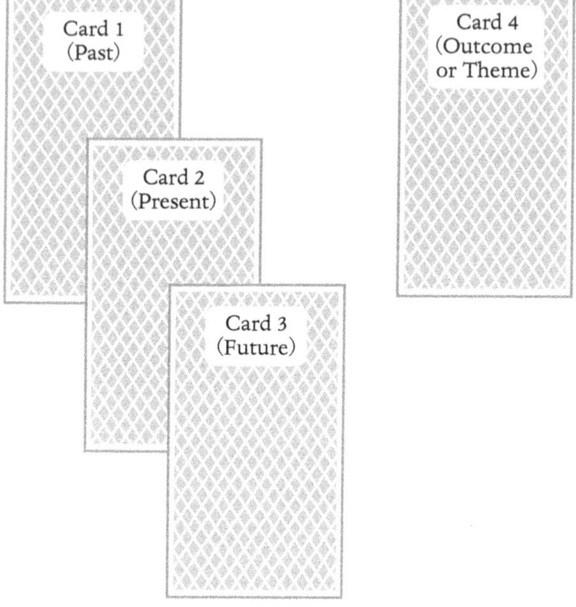

Tempest's Simple Threefold Spread (The 4-Card Pull)

The simplest spread I use (outside of pulling a single card) is one that I call the Simple Threefold Spread. This name may seem to be a bit of a misnomer, as there are 4 cards here and not 3, but the idea is that we're pulling the first three cards to represent the past (1), the present (2), and the future (3), so our view is "threefold." We then pull a fourth card for the overall outcome and theme.

The time frame for this spread doesn't have to be long either. Card 1 can represent where the querent is coming from, card 2 talks about what's going on right now because of card 1, and card 3 is the likely direction or result of card 2. Card 4 can tell us what to pay attention to or the overall effect of the other three cards.

This spread is ideal for simple, direct questions about specific things. It's not one you would use for a general spread, like "Tell me what's going on in my life." Technically you can get a lot quickly from only four cards if you have just a couple of minutes with someone, but if you're doing a reading that's 10 to 15 minutes or longer, you'll likely want to use the next spread—and if the person has any additional questions, you can use this one to clarify specifics.

A Note About the Example Readings in This Book: I didn't purposely construct any readings for this book. These are simply the cards I pulled for each question, and I'm sharing with you what came up and how I would interpret them.

Example of a Simple Threefold Spread Reading (4-Card Pull)

In this reading, the querent asked if they had made the right choice in leaving the spiritual group they were a part of. Here are the cards that were pulled:

Card 1: 10 of Swords

Card 2: Page of Cups

Card 3: 10 of Cups

Card 4: 9 of Cups

At a glance, we see that we have two 10s, a 9, and a Page. There are three Cup cards and one Sword. Now, in reference to the question, sitting in the past/origin position (card 1) is the 10 of Swords, a card that signifies the end of a cycle. Our querent was likely at the end of their rope in this spiritual group—it was not benefiting them. The Page of Cups at card 2 is where they are right now, questioning whether they made the right decision, which weighs on them emotionally. They know deep down it was the right thing to do, but leaving may have caused some drama, possibly damaging relationships and connections they did enjoy. But then we move on to card 3, the 10 of Cups: emotional fulfillment and joy. They're going to find a group that's a much better, healthier fit for them. The overall card (card 4) is the 9 of Cups. As 9s are about problem-solving and working toward completion, this card indicates they're doing a good job of processing this emotional journey and in time will recognize that they certainly made the right choice for them.

The OG Threefold Spread (The 10-Card Pull)

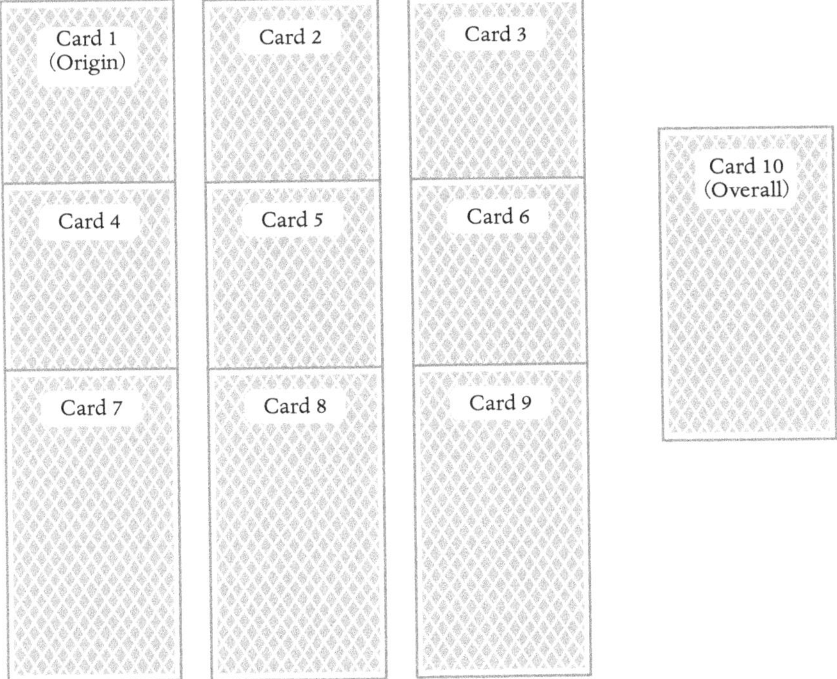

Tempest's OG Threefold Spread (The 10-Card Pull)

My main spread for more detailed readings is my Original Threefold Spread, a 10-card pull. It's like the Simple Threefold Spread in theory, but it gives us greater context and nuance. A good comparison is that the Simple Threefold is a single meal sampling, while the OG is breakfast, lunch, and dinner with a dash of dessert. By the math alone, we're referencing the whole Wheel of Fortune, so it tends to give us a nice whole view of the turning of the wheel. This is the spread I break out for most readings, especially when I ask the person if they want to look at something specific or general and they respond, "Oh, general, I guess."

That's not to say this spread is just for general readings, but it can be a good indicator of a particular area to focus on. For example, if there are a lot of Pentacles and work-related vibes showing up in the spread and the person says, "Oh yeah, there's a lot of stuff happening at work right now.

Maybe we should look at how I should proceed with XYZ project?" Using the guidance from the first spread, you can reshuffle and now pull with the focus of looking specifically at work. Don't be surprised if a few cards make a second appearance!

Here's how the 10-card OG Threefold Spread works:

Lay out three rows of three cards like a tic-tac-toe board. Cards 1, 2, and 3 make up the top row, while cards 4, 5, and 6 create the second row. The bottom row, which is closest to the querent, is made up of cards 7, 8, and 9. (If you're reading for yourself, the third row is closest to you. If you're reading for someone else, it's the farthest away from you, the reader, and closest to them, because the cards should be facing them.) Then the 10th card goes to the side, away from the main grid.

Essentially you have laid down what amounts to a simplified calendar grid of a month. Card 1 in the top left is the point of origin—where the querent is coming from. Card 9 in the bottom right is the card that is most situated in the future. Also like a calendar, we can read time across the horizontal rows as well as the vertical ones. To understand what I mean, think of your basic calendar grid, showing your average month as rows and columns of dates and days of the week. Each horizontal row is like a week on the calendar grid. Row one is the first week in the month, while row three is the last week. You also have your vertical columns, which for this example could section out as the week split up into three parts (beginning, midweek, weekend). The left row reflects the beginning of each week, whereas the right row is the end of the week. So that can give you a sense of time and order in a spread, especially if you're asking for something specific.

Sometimes for a "general" reading, the columns separate themselves not so much into neat sections of time but by area of focus. One column may indicate job or money concerns, another might focus on family or health, and the last might be about romance. When you do your initial survey of the cards, you'll notice which suits appear in the spread. If they are grouped together in the same column, that can indicate a theme or focus.

How do you tell the difference between the calendar grid effect and specific columns that represent certain themes when doing a general reading? Well, the cards will tell you that, in conjunction with your intuition. Remember, the first thing I do is look for any Major Arcana cards and where they are placed. Then I look to see what the Minor Arcana is revealing. How many Cups, Wands, Pentacles, or Swords are there? What are the numbers and faces for those cards? Then, looking at the overall configuration, is there a recurring number or theme? Maybe one row is made up of the Lovers card, the 7 of Cups, and the 2 of Cups—which are likely talking about romance. That column with the Emperor, the Ace of Pentacles, and the 8 of Pentacles is likely pointing to work. Let's look at an example of this spread to see how the cards can play.

Example of an OG Threefold Spread Reading (10-Card Pull)

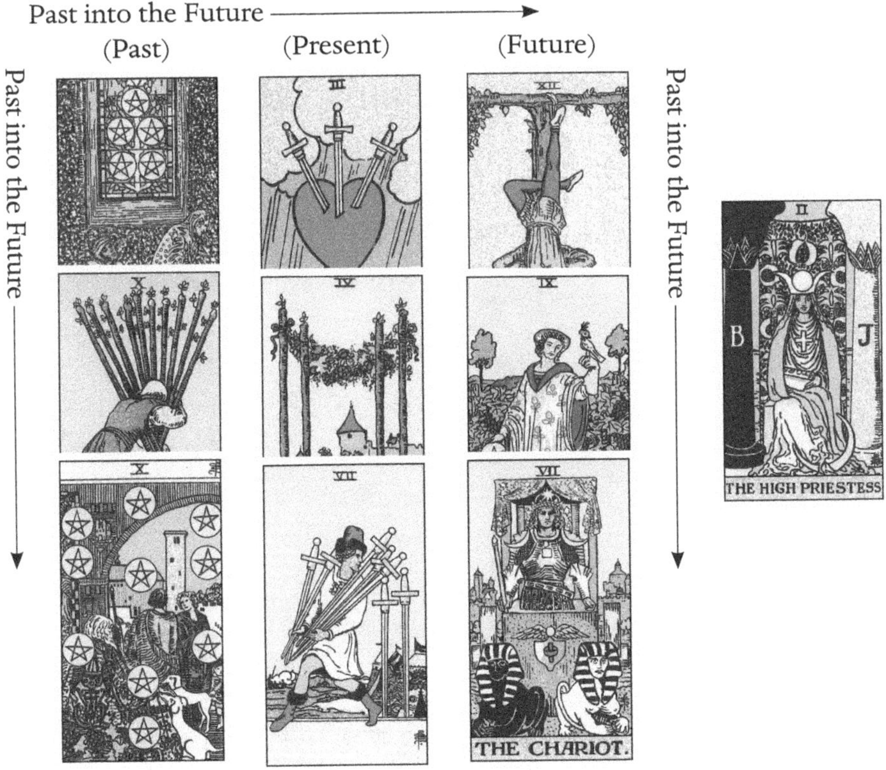

In example 1, the querent wanted a general reading of what's happening for them in the first half of the year. Here are the cards that were pulled:

Card 1 (Origin) 5 of Pentacles	Card 2 3 of Swords	Card 3 The Hanged One	Card 10 (Overall) The High Priestess
Card 4 10 of Wands	Card 5 4 of Wands	Card 6 9 of Pentacles	
Card 7 10 of Pentacles	Card 8 7 of Swords	Card 9 The Chariot	

Right off we notice that we have three Major Arcana cards. We have two 10s. There is also a 7 next to the Chariot, which is also 7. Suit-wise, there are two Swords, two Wands, and three Pentacles, which suggest that finances are an area of focus or concern for the querent. There are no Cups, which I would expect to see (the appearance of Cups) if the Pentacles pointed more to health than wealth.

The first row looks pretty rough, which is why our querent is probably wanting a reading to see what's going on and if it's going to get better. The 5 of Pentacles starting off our spread as card 1 suggests there has been some financial distress or loss. This is emphasized by the 3 of Swords (card 2) and the Hanged One (card 3). The cards indicate that the querent may have lost their job or may be suffering financial setbacks or be feeling stuck/unfulfilled in their work. But things get brighter in the second row. The 10 of Wands (card 4) indicates they are in the process of making a departure from the stagnation. It has taken some work and likely involved calling in some favors, but at the center of our spread is the 4 of Wands (card 5). Things are rebalancing, new opportunities are forming, and with the 9 of Pentacles at card 6, there is the potential for success and fulfillment. In our last row, we find the 10 of Pentacles (card 7), which confirms that finances and work relationships are going to be improving. The 7 of Swords at card 8 combined with the Chariot at card 9 means the querent not only is going in a whole new direction that they didn't think was possible at the start, but they're also on track with renewed focus and passion. The High Priestess as the overall card shows that the querent's challenge is to overcome their fears and trust their intuition.

There are some other things to notice about this spread. Our first column (cards 1, 4, 7) has a progression from 5 to 10 and 10, in particular going from a 5 of Pentacles to a 10 of Pentacles. Our second column (cards 3, 5, 8) is 3 + 4 = 7: from loss to balance to being in pursuit of their goals and overcoming the odds. The last column (cards 3, 6, 9) has two of the three Major Arcana cards in this spread. To go from the Hanged One to the Chariot is 12 − 7 = 5. The card that sits between them is a 9, but we could see that as being the solution to breaking the cycle of the 5 of Pentacles, which started us off. Also notice that the 9 of Pentacles progresses to the 10 of Pentacles as we move from the "present" row to the "future" row. Finally, we went from the 5 of Pentacles at card 1 to the Chariot at card 9. The difference between those cards is 2—which is also the High Priestess.

The Relationship Spread (A 14-Card Pull)

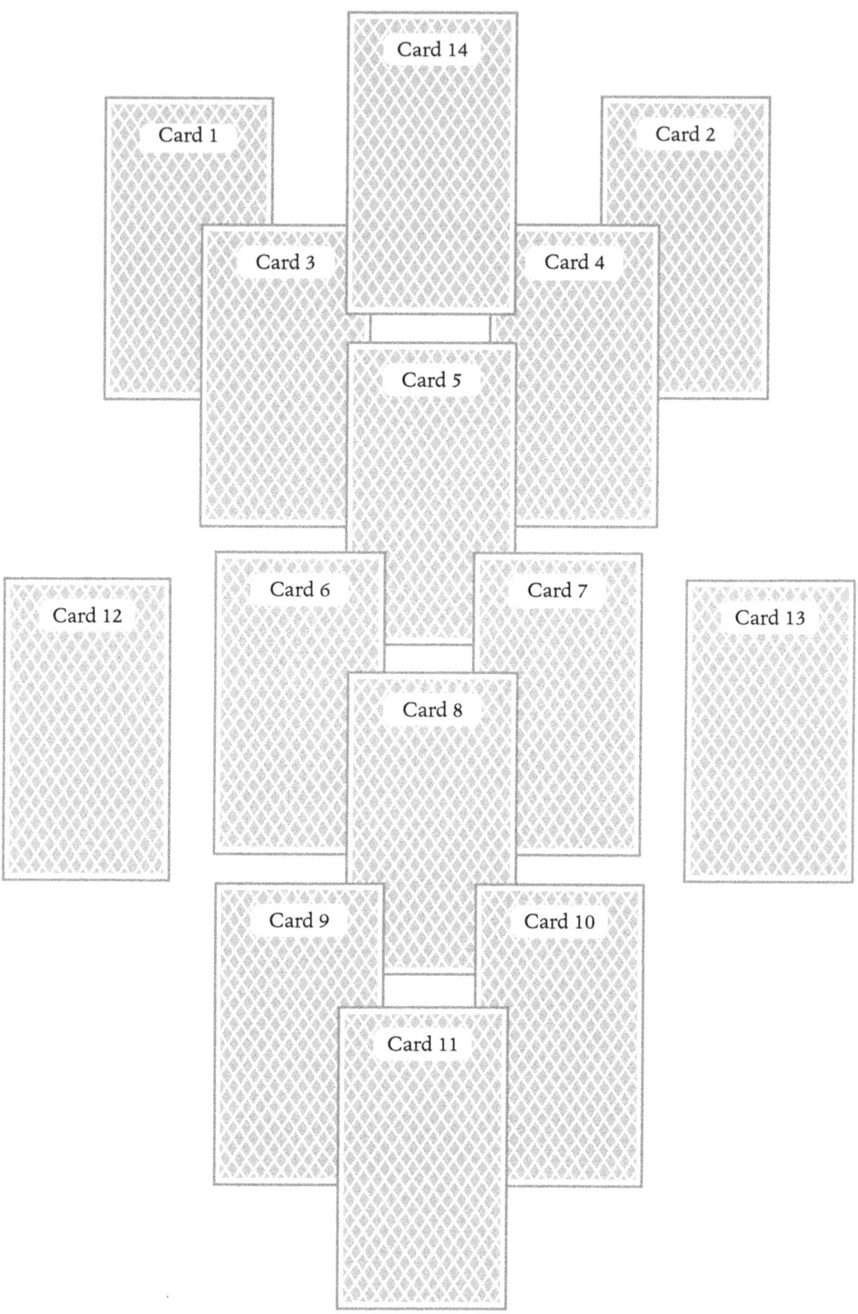

Tempest's Relationship Spread

I developed the Relationship Spread early on in my career and it's been a mainstay all these years. It's particularly handy for looking at how two people are interacting, whether we're talking romance, family, friendship, or business. At first glance, the Relationship Spread can look complicated, especially with 14 cards on the table. But once you understand what's happening, it's easy to remember and use.

First, choose which person goes on which side: left or right. If I'm reading for one half of a relationship, I ask the querent which side they want to be on. Then, by default, the other person goes in the opposite spot.

Cards 1 & 2: Where each person was coming from prior to the relationship

Cards 3 & 4: What they have brought into the relationship (origin or past)

Card 5: The state of the relationship between them as they met at that point

Cards 6 & 7: What each is bringing into the relationship (presently)

Card 8: How the relationship is progressing right now

Cards 9 & 10: Each person's development as the relationship progresses into the future

Card 11: The possible future state between the two people

Card 12: Overall card for person 1—Who are they in this relationship?

Card 13: Overall card for person 2—Who are they in this relationship?

Card 14: Overall forecast for the relationship

If your number brain is on, then you may have made the connection that, by association, this spread relates to the Temperance card. Relationships are all about give-and-take, so this spread can help us see if things feel balanced and mutual or if something's off.

Let's look at an example of the Relationship Spread in action.

Example of a Relationship Spread Reading

Our querent recently reconnected with "an old flame" from high school. (We'll call this person Pat moving forward.) They're wondering if the romantic relationship should be rekindled or should focus more on friendship. Our querent selected the left side, so the other person is on the right.

Card 1: Judgement

Card 2: 9 of Cups

Card 3: 7 of Wands

Card 4: Page of Cups

Card 5: 3 of Swords

Card 6: Queen of Swords

Card 7: 4 of Swords

Card 8: 7 of Pentacles

Card 9: Page of Wands

Card 10: King of Cups

Card 11: The High Priestess

Card 12: 6 of Cups

Card 13: Page of Swords

Card 14: Strength

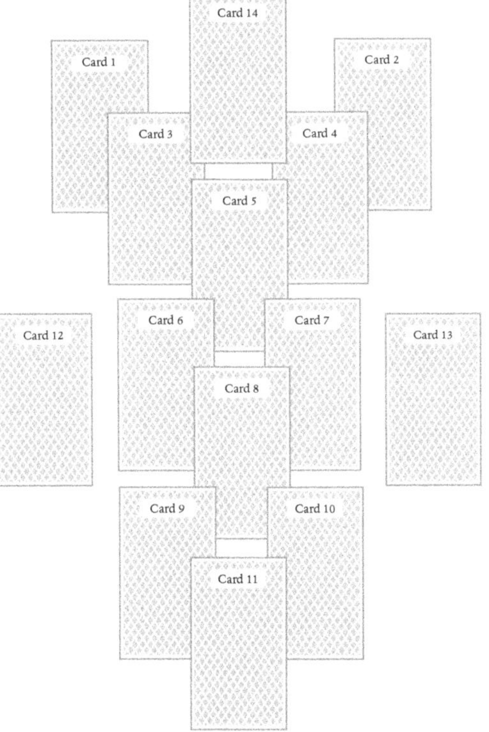

What do we see right off the bat? There are three Major Arcana cards: Judgement, the High Priestess, and Strength. We have a whopping five court cards, including three Pages, a Queen, and a King. We have two 7s, but no other repeating numbers. Suit-wise we have four Cups, two Wands, three Swords, and one Pentacle.

With the first five cards, there is a strong sense of what really went on in that initial youthful relationship. Our querent was not as much into Pat as Pat was into them—and Pat had a huge crush on our querent. Maybe our querent wasn't that attracted to Pat or was more concerned about appearances or other possible partners (Judgement and 7 of Swords), but their relationship did not last long (3 of Swords). Meeting again in adulthood, our querent is questing for nostalgia (6 of Cups) with enthusiasm (Queen of Swords). Pat is cautious (4 of Swords) and still nursing some hurt (Page of Swords). Together they meet at the 7 of Pentacles, which suggests there are some sparks and the potential for growth. Our last row suggests they will likely part ways again soon. Our querent keeps an eye on the horizon (Page of Wands), and Pat doesn't want to be rejected again (King of Cups). The High Priestess between them feels like a separation rather than a unification—like they're just not on the same page for a romantic relationship at this time. Strength is the overall card here and my eye is drawn to the lion's jaws. Instead of a gentle closure, it feels forced, like a struggle. This could be an opportunity to be honest about what happened in the past and make amends, but there's currently not a sense of compatibility for romance or friendship.

You may notice that I didn't highlight any arithmetic operations in this spread. That feels indicative of the fact that these two people simply aren't aligned well. With two 7 cards and a combination that also makes 7 (3 + 4), there is a sense that these people are in pursuit of something, but they don't have a clear idea of what they want. The fact that we have three Pages also suggests immaturity or a lack of growth when it comes to being ready to have a sincere and healthy relationship.

A more harmonious pairing typically has mirroring of similar numbers or court cards on both sides, showing balance and equal interest or effort. The cards where they meet (positions 5, 8, and 11) almost always would numerically correlate or show some sort of connection that supports their individual cards.

Designing Spreads by Number

It doesn't take a design degree to create your own Tarot spread, just a little imagination to play with shapes and stories, plus the wisdom to remember to record the design and layout so you can use it again. (Seriously, if you devise a spread that's useful to you, write that shit down. Make a diagram of the spread and be sure to legibly detail the order of the cards and their meaning. Keep this record someplace where you'll be able to easily access it in the future. You might think you're going to remember it for next time, but you won't. The ghosts of the many spreads I've created on a whim and didn't record very well can verify. Do yourself a favor and be a good archivist.)

Designing your own spreads is very useful for learning to break down and reorganize questions into a format that makes reading the cards more potent. Pretty much any question can prompt its own spread, so feel free to play!

To create your own spread, consider the following:

- What is the purpose of the spread or, more specifically, what is the question you're asking or what kind of answer are you looking for? What kind of conversation do you want to have with the cards?
- How might the question best be answered or the situation addressed? How many parts or elements need to be considered? What information or angles will help you gain insight into the situation?
- Is there a number, image, symbol, or shape that best lends itself to the layout of the spread? For example, you may use a circle-shaped spread if you're trying to figure out what's perpetuating a habitual cycle. Or you could use a spiral to help see the factors that can aid you in zooming in on a goal. A cross can bring together intersecting ideas or actions.

Here are some spreads I created for this book so that you can be inspired to create your own (but you can totally use these too!). As you can see, in some instances it's not the number of the cards in the spread that relates precisely to the archetype but rather the shape or symbolism found in the cards that does.

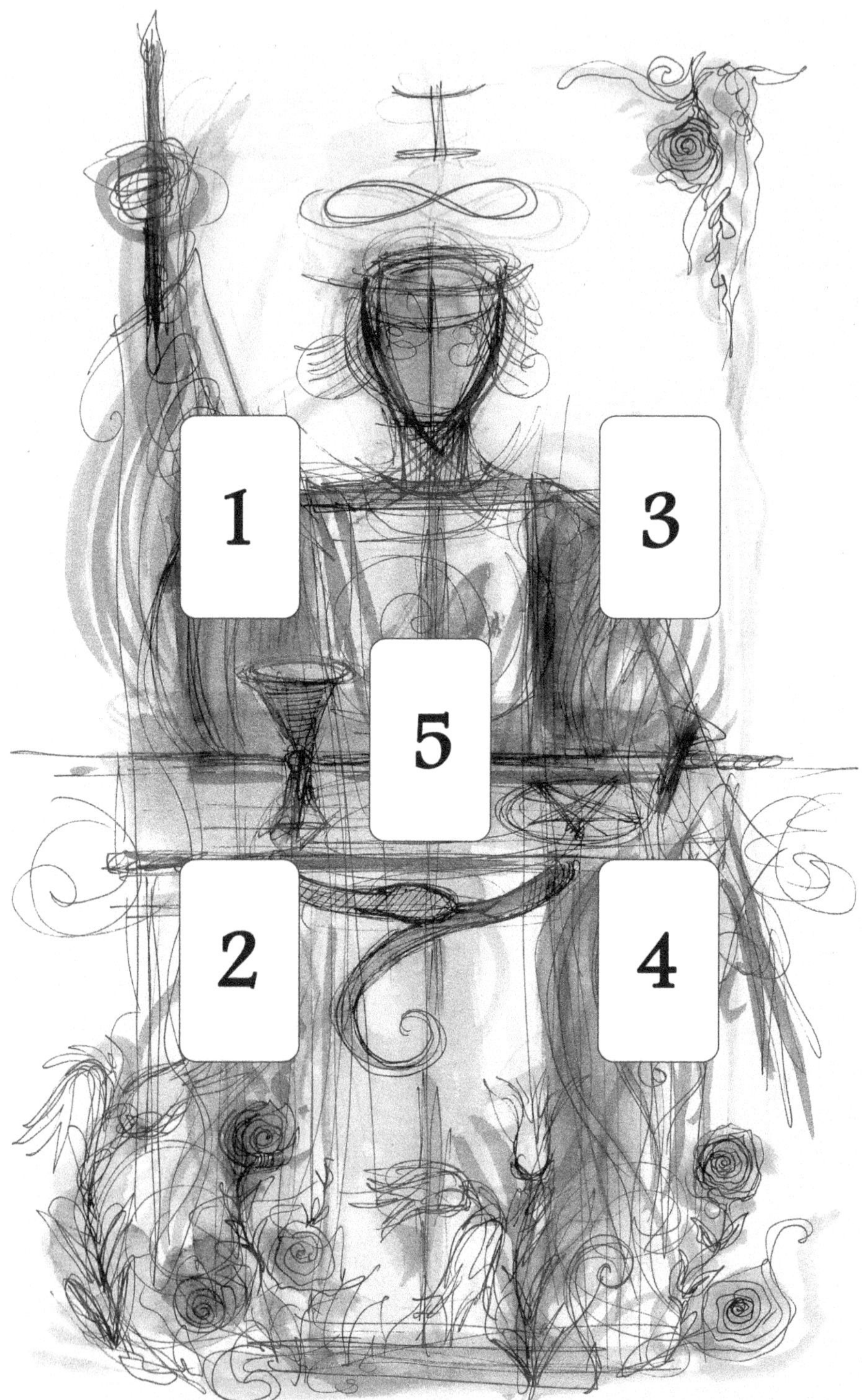

Decision of the Magician Spread

The Decision of the Magician Spread

This spread involves 5 cards and gives you a well-rounded way to examine a particular choice, to see what kind of experience you will have if you move forward with that decision.

Card 1: As Above—How will this decision affect me mentally or spiritually?

Card 2: So Below—How will this decision affect me physically?

Card 3: As Within—How will this decision affect me emotionally?

Card 4: So Without—How will this decision be received by others?

Card 5: At the Altar—What is the collective outcome, overall result, or personal impact of this decision?

The Magician is represented by the number 1, so you might be wondering why there are 5 cards. Though we are focusing on a singular choice, we are examining several specific ways this choice will influence the querent.

Not only that, but there is also the energetic gesture present in the Magician card. The alignment of cards 1 and 2 and cards 3 and 4 creates vertical lines, making the symbol for 1. Vertical lines connect north and south, the heavens and the underworlds. These two parallel vertical lines also symbolize the arms of the Magician, pointing up and gesturing downward. When I position my body to mimic the stance of the Magician, my arms don't stay static either. If I start with my left arm raised and my right arm lowered, I will switch positions to repeat the gesture mirrored.

Card 5 represents the altar, marking the horizon line between the other cards. You could place card 5 horizontally (sideways) to mimic the altar as it appears on the card, but that doesn't quite fit the energy of what we're looking for. As card 5 is the overall or outcome card, it's not going to be "crossed" by anything else. Instead, the card in this position feels like a bird's-eye view of the altar, giving a glimpse of what the future might hold from a different angle instead of straight on.

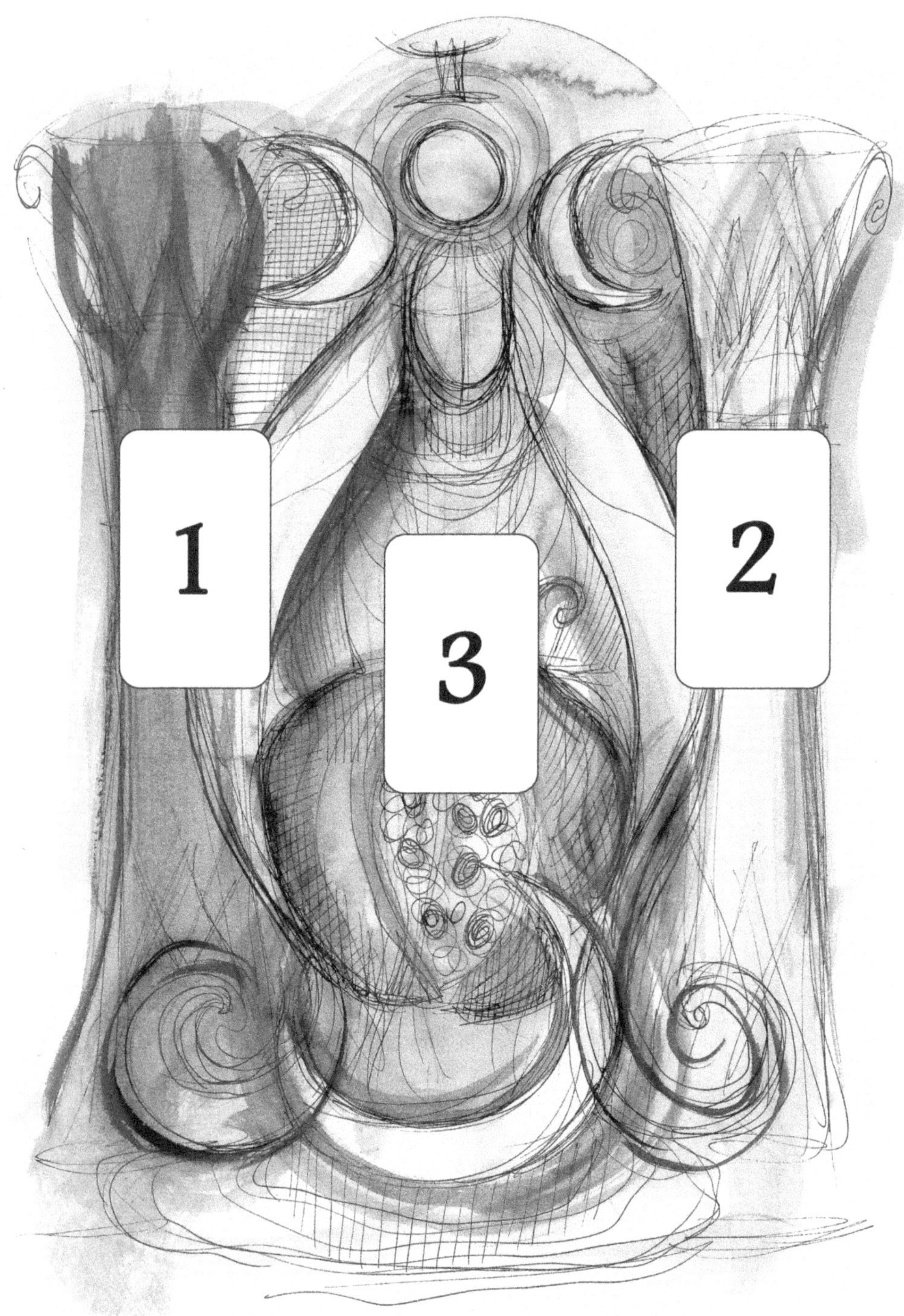

Challenge of the High Priestess Spread

The Challenge of the High Priestess Spread

This spread is a 3-card pull that can help with identifying your fears and overcoming them. It's inspired by the duality of the two pillars and the mystery that awaits us beyond the veil.

Card 1: Left Pillar—Your fears / things that block you

Card 2: Right Pillar—What can be gained if you overcome those fears / challenges

Card 3: The Pomegranate Veil—What action you can take to help you make it through

Just like in the Decision of the Magician Spread, we're not limiting the number of cards used in this spread to the number associated with the High Priestess (2). Instead, we're working with the collective symbolism found in the card. In particular, the shape is built off the two pillars and the space between them represented by the veil. Part of the mystery is that we often don't know or can't imagine what's behind the veil—and is it worth the risk to find out?

The High Priestess challenges us to face our fears and enter the mystery that awaits us. Card 1 stands in for the black pillar on our left, representing our fears and blockages. Card 2 represents the white pillar on our right. This card indicates what we might gain if we deal with the challenges shown by card 1. These two cards together create a framework for the mystery that awaits us. Card 3, representing the pomegranate veil that hangs behind the High Priestess, gives us a clue about what action we need to take to move forward.

We could also evaluate the chance of success if we follow through on the action suggested by card 3 by pulling a fourth card and placing it below or above card 3. Or we could designate this additional card to seek clarity if we're confused about the message or meaning.

Throne of the Empress Spread

The Throne of the Empress Spread

This spread is useful when you're faced with a creative block and are unsure of how to get past it. Among the gifts of the Empress are creativity and abundance—and she's a patron of the arts—so she's a good source to tap into when the muses seem too quiet or you've run out of juice.

Card 1: What's causing your block

Card 2: How to actively defeat your block

Card 3: Who is supporting you or can guide you

Card 4: Where to look for inspiration

The Throne of the Empress Spread is inspired by the pyramid or triangle shape. In theory, this shape could have been made with just three cards, but it makes the layout crowded and even hard to read if we get too literal with the laying out of the shape.

Using four cards instead helps to create a more spacious spread for ease of placement and adds more information. Also, from an architectural perspective, a pyramid may appear to have three main sides as a 2D shape, but once we bring this shape into 3D, the pyramid technically has four sides—or even five if you count the bottom! But let's not overthink this.

The first card we lay down forms the left side of the triangle and represents the source of the blockage. The second card is placed on the opposite or right side and tells us how to defeat the blockage. The third card's position forms the bottom, acting as a foundation for the triangle. This placement makes perfect sense for divining where support will come from. The last card is placed at the top or pinnacle of the triangle. Where do we often look for inspiration? Our focus is likely going to be above, at the top, or ahead of where we are headed!

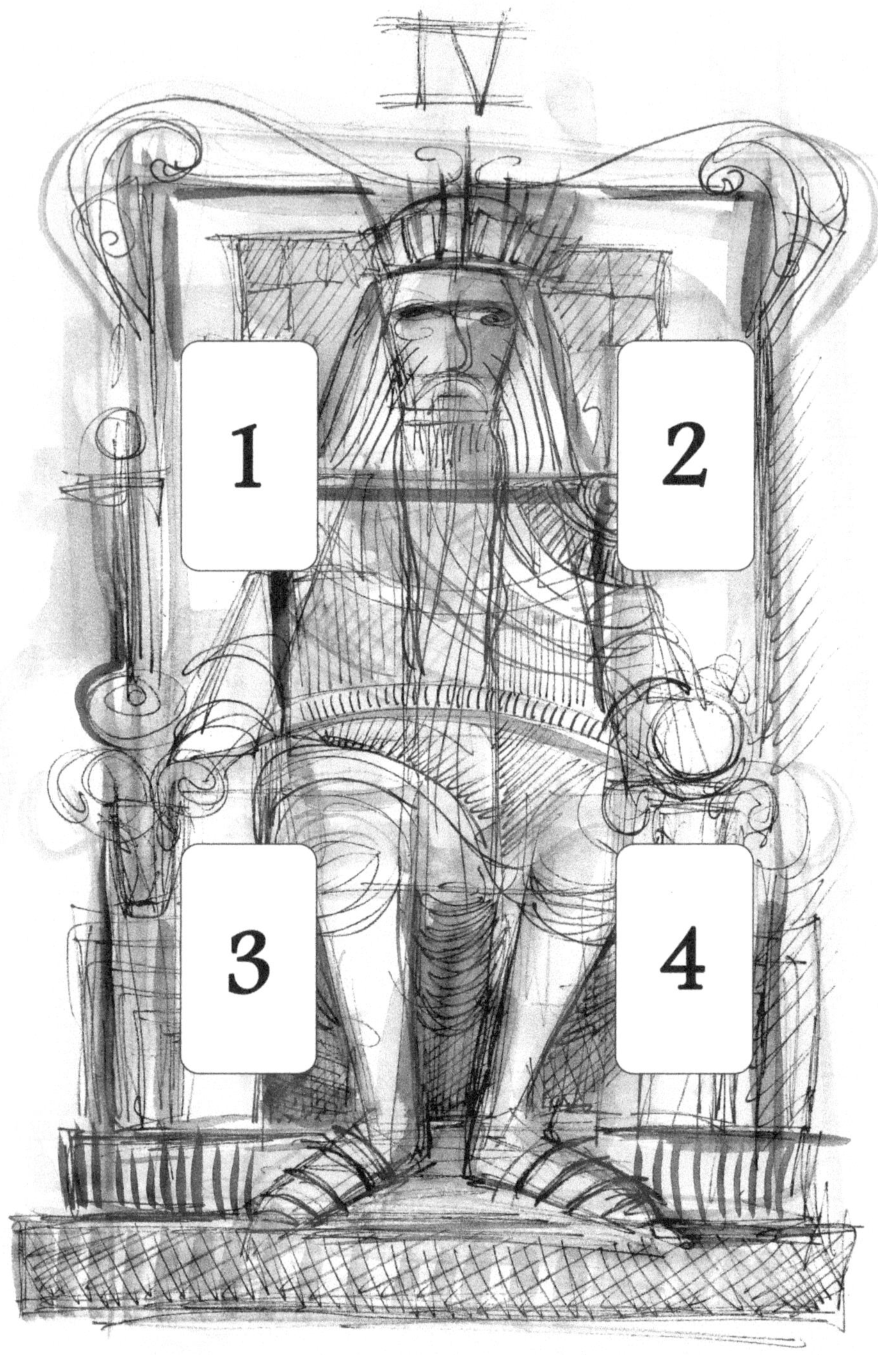

Emperor's Cornerstone Spread

The Emperor's Cornerstone Spread

As the Emperor's task is to set a strong foundation and give us guidelines to build with, this square can help formulate a structure for solving a particular work or business-related problem.

Card 1: What is the core idea I should focus on?

Card 2: What tools or skills should I utilize to accomplish this task?

Card 3: What challenges should I anticipate in the process?

Card 4: What does success look like if I choose this approach?

With the Emperor's Cornerstone Spread, we have an excellent example of where the shape of the spread, the number associated with the Emperor card, and the number of cards used to make the spread all align! We have four cards set in a rectangular placement, making the four corners that create the foundation for this reading.

Let's consider the placement of the cards as they relate to their order and meaning, as there's symbolism here as well. Cards 1 and 2 are sitting on the shoulders of the Emperor, creating a sense of weight and the need to balance things carefully. With these cards we identify not only what we should be focusing on in terms of goals but also what we have in our wheelhouse to help accomplish that task. Cards 3 and 4 rest between the knees and feet of the Emperor, giving additional support and guidance. Facing challenges can help build strength and endurance. Getting a glimpse of what success looks like can create motivation, anticipation, and momentum.

This spread prepares us for the next step, so that when the Emperor is ready to stand up and take action (the Emperor symbolically represents the querent here), the mind and body will be balanced and prepared. The foundation has been set and there are guidelines and a structure to follow.

Hierophant at the Crossroads Spread

The Hierophant at the Crossroads Spread

This 5-card spread is helpful when looking into spiritual or magical matters. The Hierophant's job is to prompt a thorough evaluation of long-held beliefs and familiar spiritual systems. To achieve growth on a spiritual or magical path, it's crucial to analyze what's working and what's causing stagnation. If you're feeling stuck, this is a good spread to use to find out why and what to do about it.

Card 1: Air / East—What is the main idea to be considered?

Card 2: Fire / South—How is this idea actively affecting me?

Card 3: Water / West—What do I need to release in order to move forward?

Card 4: Earth / North—What should I be holding on to for stability and focus?

Card 5: Spirit / Center—What truth will I find at the heart of my path?

Once again we have an alignment of the number of cards in the spread (5) with the number of the card that signifies our inspiration (Hierophant). This spread assembles the cards into a cross formation, emphasizing the idea of being at a crossroads. In many myths, the crossroads is where a variety of magical workings and rituals take place, where connections and contracts might be made with deities and spirits, and / or where we must make a choice about our future. When we stand at a crossroads, we can glimpse not only where we can go but also where we've been.

Notice the order in which the cards are meant to be consulted. We start on the right-hand side (in the east) and move clockwise around the arms of the cross, ending in the center—much like how a circle is cast in many traditions. Each card corresponds to an elemental energy that aligns with its placement: Air for thought, Fire for action, Water for fluidity, Earth for burying, and Spirit for clarity of self and truth.

While this spread is good for active divination into your path or spiritual quest, you could also use it for meditation and deeper contemplation. The Hierophant at the Crossroads Spread essentially is both an altar and a journey. What will you find at the crossroads?

Spread Design Notes

You can design a spread using pretty much any number of cards as long as it suits your purpose—and you don't run out of cards. However, the more cards you add, the more muddied things can become. An oversize spread might look impressive to an untrained eye, but it can quickly become a hot mess. Not only will it become harder to remember what card goes where and why, but it also will feel like you're trying to shoehorn everything in to twist the outcome. Using more cards doesn't necessarily equal more clarity or information.

Inspiration for spreads can be found all around. You can get inspired by flowers, herbs, trees, animals, constellations, letters, symbols—your mind is the limit. Also, just because I've provided 5 Major Arcana–inspired spreads here doesn't mean you can't devise your own spreads inspired by those cards—or any others. Find your inspiration and ask yourself, "What problem am I looking to solve and what elements or factors will help me resolve this issue?"

To quote Evvie "Evvin" Marin from their "Creating Spreadcraft" class that took place at Witch City Tarot Gathering in 2022, "If it prompts a question, it can prompt a spread." I highly recommend that you check out their fabulous work and offerings at www.interrobangtarot.com. Evvin has written some spread e-books and designed over 200 downloadable spreads that are wonderful, including their infamous WTF Tarot Spread.

Our journey isn't done yet though. Spreads and readings aren't the only activities we can do with the Tarot. In the next chapter, we will explore some other applications that involve the Tarot and playing with numbers and movement.

CHAPTER 8

Thinking Outside the Spread—More Tarot Number Ideas

There are numerous ways you can incorporate Tarot into your life that don't involve putting cards into a spread. In this chapter I'm sharing with you some of my favorite activities that involve using a Tarot deck and playing with numbers.

Divination for the Year (A Winter Solstice Ritual)

Every year either on or near the Winter Solstice, my Patreon folks and I gather on Zoom to do a solstice ritual that involves pulling cards for the New Year. The timing feels good, as we're wrapping up the calendar year and there are countless traditions around the world that incorporate divination into their wintertime celebrations.

The ritual setup is very simple. All you need is a white candle to light. A tealight is fine, but larger is fine too, or use a bayberry candle if you like that tradition. You can, of course, add as many altar items as you'd like: incense, libation, winter herbs or flowers, etc. Do what you feel called to do, but if all you can muster is a tealight for your setup, that's fine! The other necessity is a Tarot deck. We like to have a secondary form of divination as well. This can be an oracle deck, runes, the ogham, a bone- or shell-throwing set—whatever you are familiar with or are seeking to learn more about. Last but not least is something to record your findings in, ideally a small notebook you won't lose, and it doesn't hurt to take a photo of the cards with your phone just in case you put the notebook in a special place, effectively losing it for a year.

I find it's helpful to prep my notebook in advance so I'm not spending time during the ritual writing down the months. On a fresh page, label it with the new year at the top. It might seem silly right now, but if you end up doing this every year, you'll want to have an easy way to reference which year you have in front of you. On the left side of the page, I make a list of the months in consecutive order, giving each one its own line. As I like to pull from two sources, I draw a column line that splits the page vertically down the middle. I label the top of each column with the deck or tool I'm using for later reference.

After you have gathered everything you'd like to have on hand and have it assembled in a way that's both aesthetically pleasing and workable to you, do the Three Breaths exercise (page 145) to prepare. Close your eyes and take a few moments to contemplate the year that has passed. Consider what you will leave behind in the darkness and what you will bring into the light. Open your eyes and light the candle. Take your Tarot deck and begin to shuffle it. When you feel ready, pull 13 cards—one card for each month and one for the overall year. You want to pull them consecutively from the deck rather than reshuffling for every pull. Depending on how much space you have, you can simply flip over one card at a time and write it down (January = Ace of Cups, February = The Magician, etc.), or you put down three rows of four cards, like a calendar, plus one more card to the side, and turn them over one at a time to record them.

After the 13 Tarot cards have been pulled, pick up your secondary method of divination and repeat the process. Again, depending on space and which method you are using, decide how you wish to determine which month is which item.

Once you have recorded all 26 pulls in your mini spreadsheet, the next step is doing some quick note-taking on each item. In the pages following the chart, I write down the month and my initial thoughts on the Tarot card and my other method. Do *not* go instantly for the little white book that came with your Tarot deck. Don't question what pops into your head either. Just write down whatever comes, then go to the next set until you have finished all your pulls. You can always go back later if you want to write down the more traditional meanings or keywords, but for now, trust your intuition.

Once you are finished writing and are ready to end the ritual, blow out the candle and put your stuff away.

Now that you've done the ritual, the next important step is to actually make a habit of referencing what you've pulled. The best way to do this, I find, is to consult your notebook at the beginning or end of each month. Look at what you pulled and what you thought it meant at the time, and consider what you think now. In February, you will be able to look back at January, consider what the messages are for February, and even peek ahead at March. On my Patreon Zoom, each month we have a "Tarot Time" theme for one of our weekly gatherings. At the start of each of these sessions, folks can share their thoughts about how the pulls turned out and what is going on in their lives. It has become a very insightful and powerful practice for a lot of people!

If you're coming across this idea and the Winter Solstice is a long way away, there's nothing preventing you from pulling a card for each month left in this current year and one overall. No time like the present to consider the future!

What's Your Tarot Card for the Year?

If 13 cards for the year seems a bit overwhelming to you—or maybe you just know you're not going to be good about checking in monthly with yourself—there are simpler options to consider.

One method is to consider what Tarot card aligns for the year in general. To do this, you simply add up the numbers. For example, 2026 is $2 + 0 + 2 + 6 = 10$. You have the choice of reducing 10 down to 1, which means the card for the year would be the Magician, or you can leave it at 10, making 2026 the Wheel of Fortune. Or, playing with the math a little more when you have double digits, you can use the first sum as the overall theme for the year and the reduced number as how to best approach the year. The upside of this approach is that you can get a general sense of what the year could bring on a larger scale. The downside is that this calculation may not feel as personal for you.

One way to get a more personalized method for your journey this year is to add your birthday to the mix. I was born on June 13, so for 2026 I'd add 6 + 1 + 3 + 2 + 0 + 2 + 6 = 20. That gets me the Judgement card for 2026 or, if reduced to 2, the High Priestess. The way I might interpret those two cards is that I'm reaching the end of a cycle or heading toward a worthy resolution that may involve recognition and greater understanding. The High Priestess reminds me to face my fears and not be afraid of exploring new territory.

One more method of associating Tarot with this year of your life is to simply add up your age. For example, if you're currently 24 years old, you're having a "6" year (2 + 4 = 6), which means the Lovers card. Therefore, the consideration for the year is finding out what's most important to you emotionally and what sets your heart in motion in all aspects of your life. Note that the next year will be the Chariot and so forth, until you reach a new decade.

Whatever method you use, you could place representations of the card or cards on your altar so you can honor that energy throughout the year. If you have just one deck, you could print out images of those cards and frame them or draw/assemble your own interpretations. Or, if you have multiple decks but maybe don't use one regularly, you could pull the cards from that deck for altar work.

The Cards as Archetypes for Problem-Solving and Spellcraft

We have been discussing the Tarot mainly in terms of divination throughout this book, but there are so many other applications. The following is an interesting concept that I feel straddles the line between spellcraft, archetype exploration, and affirmations. Since the cards of the Major Arcana represent human archetypes and concepts, we can use them as goals for our own personal development. Not only do they work as an abstract model, but when we consider the math, their numbers can also help craft a path for us to get there.

For example, let's say you are seeking justice in your life, whether because of legal issues, unfair treatment, or some other area where you need resolution and rebalancing. You know that Justice sits at 11. What components from the other Major Arcana would best help you arrive at 11? If you're looking for speedy justice in your favor, then you might seek out the Chariot at 7 for directness and speed and the Emperor at 4 for foundation and fair ruling. If it's something of a more personal nature, then you could select the Empress at 3 for sovereignty and creativity and Strength at 8 for support that affects you—mind, body, and soul.

Okay, so you've picked a goal card and selected two or more cards to help build your path to that card. Now what? Here are some suggestions, depending on your comfort level.

Option 1: Pull the necessary cards from the deck and place them on your altar for meditation work. If you don't have an altar,[26] you could lean the cards on your bedroom dresser, tuck them into a bathroom mirror, or set them any other place where you can see them on a daily basis. Keep them up for as long as necessary, but don't forget about them. Engage with the cards on a regular, ritualized basis to help connect with and empower your goals.

Option 2: At the next full moon, set the cards on your altar, carefully propped up. Place them in a line like an equation, with the goal archetype on the right side and the other cards on the left so they "add up." Choose a votive candle for each card. Starting with the smallest number, light the candle for that card, do the Three Breaths exercise (page 145), and say or chant the words you associate most with that card as you focus on it and the candle flame visually. Repeat this pattern for each card until you have completed the whole equation. You can let the candles burn for as long as they are safe and attended, but if you need to blow them out, that's fine.

26. Want to know more about altars? Check out *The Witch's Altar* from myself and Jason Mankey, which contains everything you need to know about setting up and maintaining an altar in one handy and accessible little book.

Option 3: Devise a simple moving meditation that moves energetically through all your chosen cards, building from the smallest to the largest number. This movement can be as small as something you do with your hands or as big as something that involves your whole body. Make this movement part of your daily practice until the goal is accomplished. For example, if your goal is the Chariot and you've selected the Empress and the Emperor, you can draw a triangle in the air to represent the Empress, then draw a square around it for the Emperor. Then, with both hands, direct energy forward as if you were snapping the reins to horses on a chariot. Boom!

Option 4: This is similar to option 3, but instead of creating a moving meditation, use a symbol from each of the cards to create a combined sigil that you can apply to a candle or your body, make into something to wear, or use however else may be best aligned with your goal.

Dance the Tarot for Daily Meditation and Path Building

In the previous exercise, I recommended using Tarot-based movement for spellcraft. But maybe you don't have a spell-related goal and just want to move your body. Pulling a Tarot card to dance—either one a day or one per week—is a great way to be in motion as well as discover more about each card in the process.

I recommend selecting a dedicated deck to be used specifically for this purpose. In particular, you will likely want to choose a deck where the art involves human figures, so it's easier to model the poses and imagine the story. I also suggest that you edit the deck down so it's just the Major Arcana and the court cards. (Just don't forget where you put the rest of the cards for when you want to reunite the deck.)

The idea is to shuffle the edited deck and select a card to work with. Look carefully at the pose of the figure (or figures). Start by trying to copy that pose and consider how this person may move. What shapes do you see in the card? If it's a court card, how does the suit affect their personality and energy? What does it mean to hold a cup, a stave, a sword, or a sphere?

How would you move it around? Play with the shapes and movements, focusing on how your body feels instead of how it may look in a mirror. Depending on your stamina and ability to move, this exercise could last just a couple of minutes or you could make it a whole full-length workout!

You may also be inspired to make a playlist. Perhaps you assign a certain song to a particular suit or kind of court card, or maybe each Major Arcana card has its own song. Or you can work with whatever music consistently moves you. Keep track of your songs in whatever music app you prefer so that you can summon your music whenever you want to.

If there's a particular archetype in the Major Arcana that you wish to embody in your magical practice, dancing that card is a means to path building. Embodying the energy of that pose for a few minutes each day will reveal a deeper understanding of the archetype.

By the way, if you look at my YouTube channel (@LTZWitch), you will find several "Witchual Workouts" that are inspired by Tarot cards.

I hope you find these suggestions inspiring and try them out. There are even more ways you can incorporate Tarot into your practice. In fact, some of my friends and folks I admire have written whole books on the subject. In the Suggested Resources section I've included some other books you may want to explore. Give yourself the freedom to experiment with your own ideas—you never know what will work best for you until you give it a try. You may even surprise yourself!

CHAPTER 9
Tarot Talk!

Every time I teach my "Tempest's Tips for the Tarot" workshop, people are excited about using the numbers, but they usually still have some questions about Tarot in general that exist outside of what we've covered here. Consider this chapter the Q&A section, taking place in the Hermit's cave. Let's have a chat and enjoy some snacks as we cover some of the issues and questions you might have about Tarot reading.

Reading for Yourself

Sometimes it's harder to read for yourself than for someone else. We can be too close to the source and have a hard time deciphering what the cards are telling us. It's difficult not to be biased about what we see for ourselves—and even more challenging to practice accountability. By accountability, I mean when you pull a card you don't like and then decide to pull another card, or reshuffle and pull some more, all in an effort to get a better pull. We're less likely to do that when we're reading for someone else because it's *their* life and it's often easier to be more objective. Plus you've got a witness when you're reading for someone else! That's why it's vital to be specific about what you're looking for and be honest with yourself when it's just you and the cards (and the spirits, gods, and ancestors ...).

Q. What's the Best Way to Phrase My Question?

Collect your thoughts and consider how to receive the most clarity. This process involves not only phrasing your question to reflect that goal but also selecting a spread that makes sense. If I'm trying to choose between two or more options as my best course of action, I will be clear about what those options are and assign places in the spread that represent each. For example, let's say I have two conflicting events and I'm not sure which one to choose. My question would be, "Which is the best course of action: Event A (card 1), event B (card 2), or neither (card 3)?" If I pull the Sun for 1, the Tower for 2, and the 4 of Swords for 3, the choice is pretty obvious that, if I had to choose an event, event A would be the ticket.

If you have a specific situation but are having a hard time seeing options or answers, you may want to ask, "What's my best course of action for this scenario?" or "What am I missing regarding this situation?"

I think good phrasing comes down to considering what will give you the most guidance and selecting a spread that helps you find that information. Think about these questions regarding what you want to look into: "What should I know?" "What's blocking me?" "Who can help me?" "What are the choices I can see?" Sometimes when you work backward from your goal, you realize what information is missing and what you really need to know. This knowledge helps to clarify your question and hone in on what you're seeking insight into.

There are times when you're just looking to get the temperature of what's going on and find out if there's anything you should know about it. That's fairly open-ended for a question, but you can always dive deeper into something that comes up. You can also do a reading around a general focused topic, such as work, family, relationships, etc. A daily pull is along the same lines—you're just seeing what the deck has to say.

Regardless of how you end up phrasing your question, you should have a solid sense of what you're looking for *before* you start shuffling. Know *why* you're pulling the cards, whether it's general or specific!

Q. Is It Okay to Do a Daily Reading?

Absolutely! But you should have a clear purpose for why you're doing a daily reading. Good questions for daily readings are things like this:

- "What should I know about today?" (morning reading)
- "What lesson should I remember about today?" (evening reading)

A single card pull that you can meditate on is also a good idea. It technically goes under "What should I know about today?" but can also be used as an effective way to explore your deck card by card. I also feel it's harder to argue with a single card.

Q: How Do I Get Out of My Own Head?

Try ritualizing your reading experience. Instead of just pulling your deck off the shelf and throwing down some cards, you can make the process a ritual so it shifts your consciousness. Clear a space for your reading area, set up a nice cloth, a candle, and some incense, and maybe play some soft music. These actions and elements speak to your senses, signaling that something special is happening. Depending on your practice, you could cast a circle and call in spirits, deities, or ancestors if you'd like. Settle yourself, do the Three Breaths exercise (page 145), and begin to shuffle. Clarify in your mind or speak aloud your question. Be specific about how you will do your spread and lay the cards out almost as if you were reading for someone else. What comes to mind? What advice would you give? You may wish to write down your thoughts and impressions, so have a journal handy. Having to put into words what you're seeing often makes it harder for your brain to argue with or second-guess what the cards are saying. Making card reading a ritual may seem like a lot of work, but if you're struggling with reading for yourself, this approach is a good way to train your brain to be more objective.

Q: What If I Use an App Versus Pulling a Physical Card for a Daily Pull?

I personally prefer to hold the cards in my hands versus using an app. I like the feel of the cards, the movement of the shuffle, and selecting the card myself. But I have plenty of friends who use phone-based apps instead for their daily pulls and swear by them. I'm also the kind of person who prefers to read a paperback versus a book on my tablet, so it's mainly a personal preference for the tactile experience. I also find it easier on my eyes—but I know reading on phones and tablets helps a lot of people who have trouble with physical books. It's not a matter of what's more magical or special but rather what works best for you and your body.

Q. This One Card Keeps Coming Up Again and Again—and Flying Out of My Deck at Me! What Does It Mean??

Whether you're dealing with an oracle deck or Tarot, the deck is trying to tell you something and you've just not been getting it or paying attention. Are you asking the same question again and again, or does one specific card seem to be coming out all the time? Sit down with the card and really look at it. What do you see? Analyze the colors, symbols, and imagery. What do you feel when you look at this card? How does that relate to the traditional or intended meaning of the card?

Also, sometimes a card is just damaged (bent edge, rough corner, some other flaw), so it keeps separating from the pack. This is not necessarily a message, but is far more likely to simply be an exercise in physics.

Reading for Others

Reading for other people often invites a whole other set of issues, especially when we start charging money for readings so it becomes a business. Suddenly you're not just "slinging cards," but are playing a role in other people's lives that you may not have expected.

Q. What's the Best Way to Gain Experience Reading for Others?

As I mentioned back in the introduction, I started giving readings online for friends in chat rooms and then in person for folks I knew. From there, people wanted to hire me for parties and festivals, so I gained more experience that way (and was paid). Now I recommend that folks find or organize reading groups, either in person or online. This can be a meetup where everyone agrees to read for each other and give feedback. It's a safer environment and you're not in active competition with professional readers, flying by the seat of your pants. I'd recommend practicing for *at least* six months to a year before deciding if you want to read professionally.

Keep in mind that every person learns at a different rate, plus you now know that reading is more than just memorizing cards, so your mileage may vary.

Q. I Would Like to Read Professionally. How Much Should I Charge?

You need to know what's being offered in your area and get on board with the going rate. Check out local psychic fairs, festivals, shops, etc. to see what other people are charging. Don't undercut other readers. If you offer more services, don't be afraid to charge more either.

I produce several events a year that feature a readers' row or garden, with anywhere from six to a dozen readers who set up in a special designated area so they can offer their services in a semiprivate, quiet setting. For a few of these events, I compile information sheets on each reader that give potential clients a little background and detail their offerings. The readers are fairly consistent with keeping their rates on par with their peers—maybe at max a $5 difference for similar offerings—and the rates go up on a regular basis. We live in a small region with a high population, so everyone knows everybody else. It's better to build a healthy relationship with your fellow readers than try to undercut or undermine them. As a reader, I've often recommended other readers I trust if I couldn't make a gig or if they needed multiple readers. Everyone wins when we support each other.

Another important thing when reading professionally is knowing the laws in your town or city. Many places in the United States have archaic laws on the books that forbid "fortune-telling," even if they're not always actively enforced.[27] Some towns allow certain kinds of readings but may

27. At the time I am writing this book, Beck, who owns the Serpent's Key in Hanover, Pennsylvania, has a lawsuit involving local law enforcement that has been going on for two years now regarding a law from 1861. This law makes it a misdemeanor to "pretend, for gain or lucre, to tell fortunes or predict future events" using cards, tokens, or other methods. Beck's lawsuit argues that the law is discriminatory and outdated, violating First Amendment rights.

require special licensing for others (such as palmistry). Other towns issue only a certain number of permits per year. So do your research!

Also, if you're going to go professional and want to make this a business, do it properly. You'll need a good headshot for promotion, a short biography so people can learn more about who you are and what you do, a set list of prices and services, a way for folks to contact you, and a means to collect money (if you're not working through a storefront that handles this for the readers). Keep a record of your readings, track your receipts (space rental, processing fees, decks and other tools), register as a business entity if needed, and file your taxes. I know, it's not glamorous, but I've known far too many full-time readers who didn't operate officially as a business. It may have made them a fair bit of money under the table, but it also caused them a lot of headaches when trying to rent or buy a home, get credit, etc. So be smart and responsible!

Q. Should I Charge for Readings in the First Place?

If you're offering a service and presenting yourself as a professional, you should be compensated for your time and energy. That might mean money is exchanged or something is bartered. There are many reasons for this,[28] but one of the main ones is that people rarely value something they've gotten for free. The other is that you're setting up a bad business model if there are other readers in your area and devaluing everyone's work. It's also important to set boundaries, as some people may take advantage of your time and energy and think they can get a reading whenever they want, even people you consider friends or family. That said, I do on rare occasion gift readings to certain people, but it's not something I do often or on a public level.

28. I have a whole workshop called "The Business of Witchcraft" that goes into extensive detail about magical practitioners and dealing with money. It covers artists, musicians, readers, other service providers, events, shops, etc.

Q. What If Someone Isn't Taking Their Reading Seriously?

When you're reading for the public, especially at street festivals and parties, you're going to experience a wide range of querents. Some will be very serious, others curious, and others are just doing it for a lark. If you're being hired to read at a party, you're essentially viewed as entertainment or a curiosity, so it's going to come with the territory. However, I find that when given a short, accurate reading, the unserious querent quickly changes their tune and becomes invested in the process. A lot of folks hide being nervous or even scared to get a reading with bravado when egged on by their friends. If you make them feel at ease and give them insight, they become more comfortable or even amazed. To me, it's a wholly different animal from someone who is deliberately trying to be a dick. (See the next question.)

Q. What If Someone I'm Reading for Is Very Guarded or Even Antagonistic?

Reading for a difficult querent can be a very stressful situation. Sometimes a person is guarded simply because they're uncomfortable with the whole situation and/or aren't very aware of their own body language. If they're put at ease, then the shields tend to come down. There are several ways to help folks relax. Here are some things I like to do:

- Ask them if it's their first reading, and if so, give them a quick rundown of what they can expect. This talk can include the technical aspects, like "We can start with a general reading and get more specific from there, unless there's something in particular you have in mind?" You might also reassure them that Tarot reading isn't doom and gloom—it's about gaining insight and problem-solving. A little introduction like this is a handy thing to have in your mental toolbox for a variety of clients.
- I often have a few items on my reading table that people can hold, such as the hematite sphere I mentioned earlier, a cute little stuffed animal, or a figurine that's comfortable to grasp.

- Invite them to take some deep breaths with you for grounding and focus.
- If they don't have an issue with smells, I may invite them to try an anointing oil or cleansing spray to prepare for the reading (also available at my table). Some people really like the ritual aspect of this task and it takes their mind off things for a bit.

But some people are guarded to the point of antagonizing the reader. Thankfully I can count those on one hand, and funnily enough they were all the same sign. But the fact that I remember those two or three readings twenty-plus years later says something about the experience. I was quite young and struggling financially, and I especially wanted to make every client happy. The first time it happened, I struggled through the reading (internally) and they seemed fine and happy at the end. But it shook me. It also didn't help that at the time I was reading at a mall shop where business was slow in general. So I felt I had to deal with this person because both the shop and I needed the money. The second time it happened, I was working at the Psychic Eye and very much in demand. This time, I recognized the signs and just stopped the reading before we really got started. I told them that I didn't think we were a good fit, but they should try one of the other readers instead who was available. It wasn't worth the fifteen minutes of my day to deal with them, nor the resulting head monkeys.

You might say, well, if I'm offering a service to the public that is supposed to help people, I should deal with the difficult people too. But I think we all have our version of what "difficult" is, and I'd rather save my time and energy for someone who generally wants and needs a reading versus someone who thinks it will be fun to be an asshole. I've also discovered that, whether I'm doing readings, making custom art for people, or being hired for performances, I need to follow my gut. Every time I've ever thought, "Well, we could really use the money," and went against my gut, the experience was a shit show. Not only are my sanity and time worth protecting, but I've found that the money will come some other way. Take care of you.

Q. What If Someone Doesn't Believe What I'm Telling Them?

I call this "a them problem." If I had a dollar for every time someone said, "I'm not sure if this is me or what this is in relation to" and then came back a little while later with, "OMG, you were so right!" I'd have a nice thick stack of cash. Be confident in what you're reading and trust that they will figure it out, even if it hasn't connected right at the moment. Some people just have short-term blockages, no matter how precisely and accurately you explain what you're seeing.

Q. Can I Read for Someone Who Isn't Present?

Is it ethical to read for someone who isn't giving explicit consent? To what extent is someone else popping up in your querent's reading much different from doing a reading on that person? What about when the dead come through to deliver a message or the querent wants to know about someone who is deceased? If you see a therapist, do you talk about other people in your life during your appointment? There's a lot of gray ethical area here and I think it comes down to intent and what information is shared with whom and how.

When I was reading full-time, I would often do readings that involved people who weren't present. In fact, most of the times I've used my Relationship Spread, only one person involved was physically present. Frankly, it can get a bit awkward if both people are present. With the Relationship Spread, the focus is more on what the querent needs to know about their part in the relationship than anything else. We're not spying on someone else but rather getting a glimpse into what part they're actively playing in the combined relationship. I've also done some readings best classified as "let's check in on so-and-so," and the majority of those readings were more about peace of mind for the querent and how they could best support that person in their own lives. They were often family-related readings for children, parents, and other family members. They're typically seeking insight into how to help navigate problems at school, deal with family crises, handle health situations, etc. These situations feel different than questions like "Will he leave his wife for me like he promised?" or "Who is she cheating on me with?" I feel those questions are best redirected back to the querent, with a focus on helping them deal with their insecurity, guide them to build better relationships, and direct attention to other things that are in their own hands.

Q. A Client Keeps Asking the Same Question Over and Over Again and/or Is Constantly Wanting Readings. What Do I Do?

This scenario is probably one of the most exhausting things about being a reader. And I'd say probably nine times out of ten, it's about a relationship—and rarely a healthy one. The querent is obsessed and grasping at straws, wanting to hear the best outcome possible. As humans, we want to give each other hope, but the reality is the querent is likely stuck in a loop and is rarely doing anything to actually improve their well-being. They're just hoovering up the hope and waiting for fate to deliver. They're addicted to the experience.

I had people wanting readings every week or even almost every day. I'd handle things a lot differently today than I did back then when it comes to these clients. I'd enforce a strict timetable for readings, as not much can change in just a day or a week or even a month—especially if the person isn't taking responsibility themselves. I'd also refocus the readings more strongly back on the querent, with suggestions on what they could do. The reality is that in most cases the client will seek out another reader to get what they *think* they need and they'll ignore the assistance you try to give them. The end result is likely one less client perhaps, but then you have room and energy for more folks you can help.

See if you can ask them to reframe their own question to help guide them toward being proactive and responsible for their own outcomes. This approach may help to break the loop and enable them to perhaps see other options, ideas, and possibilities. But to be honest, the chances of this happening are slim. For years after I stopped offering readings to the public, I would still receive emails from some of those clients trying to get a reading. I have no doubt that if I still had access to my old Yahoo account, there would be recent emails in there.

I know some readers who recognize the fact that if they're not the one giving that person a reading, they're going to go somewhere else anyway, so they say, "Why not make that money?" They may also see themselves as a lifeline for that person, exhausting as it is. Is that taking advantage of someone's weakness or is it providing a service? Frankly, I don't think it's healthy for either party.

Another thought is to consider setting up a policy that restricts the frequency that someone can get a reading from you and make that information clear. This approach works best if you're the one doing the scheduling or setting up the system. It can also work if you're reading at a shop that recognizes these issues and respects you and therefore doesn't force clients on you. You can, of course, take on a reading outside of the schedule if someone's having an emergency, but I wouldn't put that information out there because some people will abuse that angle.

Q. How Do I Deliver Very Bad News?

The short answer is you don't. Keep in mind that you're reading the Tarot, but you are not the Fates themselves. We've all seen bad stereotypical representations of Tarot readers in movies and on TV shows where the reader predicts that terrible things will happen. This drama is a means to move the plot along and is *not* a model to follow with actual querents. Now, I'm not saying to tell everyone that everything is peachy, made of unicorns or covered in roses. But unless it's a developing situation that the client *is already aware of*, your job is to help them navigate future rough waters, not use predictive dramatic detail to say exactly what you think is going to happen. Because while you're getting a glimpse of something coming up, it's not likely you're seeing the whole picture. If you see something health-related that looks concerning, you might want to direct them to schedule a checkup soon as preventive care. Think about what actionable things a person might be able to do to prevent or prepare for rough times. Be careful of giving false hope, but also keep in mind that nobody is doomed.

Q. Is There Such a Thing as Client Privacy and Confidentiality When It Comes to Tarot Readings?

Nobody is signing a HIPAA form when they're getting a reading,[29] but it's best not to be a gossip and to keep what happens at the reading table between you and the querent. I have seen readers blab online or at events about some of their more dramatic readings and often there are far too many specific clues that could lead a querent to recognize themselves. It's super cringe. Be considerate and respect your clients.

There are occasions where, with a regular client, you may want to keep a log that details their appointment schedule and any important information that you may want to refer back to. The log should be kept private and secure, with a code name or abbreviation for the client.

Q. What About Privacy and Safety for Myself?

As we've already talked about, some clients can get obsessive and there are far too many stories of readers being stalked. It's important to look after your own privacy and safety from the start. Many readers use an alias for their public name to keep their personal and professional lives separate. You can use a Google number instead of giving out your actual phone number and create a separate email and social media. Refrain from sharing specific details about your life with clients, including the names of family members and partners or where you live.

And I'm going to emphasize this again: Set up boundaries and maintain them. Obviously not every client is going to be a problem or a creeper, but it's easy to feel close to someone when you're discussing intimate details of someone's life. This feeling goes both ways. What I am going to say next might sound harsh, but either you can have clients or you can have friends. I'm not talking about situations where you're doing a one-off reading for a longtime friend, but about those folks who come to you for readings first and the lines start to become blurred. I have made this mistake several

29. Though if you read for someone who is a celebrity, you may be the one signing an NDA.

times, and I truly wish someone had shared this wisdom with me when I was starting out.

Deck Tech

After all this talk about people, what about the deck itself? Let's cover some common issues that you might face when dealing with a physical deck.

Q. Someone Gifted Me a Deck and I'm Not Sure What to Do with It.

When someone gifts you a new deck, there are a few scenarios:

- If the deck appeals to you, open it up and use it!
- If the deck doesn't appeal to you, rehome it with someone who will enjoy it, perhaps just not directly in front of the gift giver.
- If it's a copy of a deck you already have and love a lot, you might want to hold on to it as a backup for when your first deck wears out, or you could share the love with someone else and pass it along. But seriously, hold on to that backup deck.

What if someone gifts you a beloved used deck? Maybe it came from someone who passed away, or maybe it's from a friend or family member's collection. If the deck has meaning for you because of who it belonged to, then honor them by connecting with the deck (as we talked about in chapter 6) and using it as part of your own practice. I believe magical tools should be utilized when possible versus languishing on the shelf gathering dust. Or, if the deck isn't in the best condition, consider placing it on an ancestor altar or in a similar place of honor. If you're not familiar with the person the deck belonged to and the deck doesn't appeal to you, then help it find a new home.

Q. What Should I Do If I Stop Connecting with a Deck?

If it's a deck you really love but it just doesn't seem to be working for you, I recommend cleansing the deck and putting it aside for a while. Try reading with other decks and see if any of those are working better for you. It's natural to cycle through decks depending on your mood, the season, what inspires you, and the kinds of issues you are currently doing readings for.

If a deck isn't particularly special to you or just doesn't seem like a good match, you can always sell it or give it away. There are lots of groups online for the trading and selling of decks. There may also be a local meetup or a card swap at a festival where you can help the deck find a new home. I particularly love the swaps because the decks are often already opened, so you can look through them and try them out and everyone can go home with something if they want.

Q. Oh No! Disaster Has Happened! What Do I Do with My Damaged Deck?

Well, if you're me, you carefully wrap your beloved, dearly departed deck in a lovely fabric bag and stow it on your shelf in a place of honor. Then every couple of years, you pull it down, look at its mangled remains, sigh, and wrap it back up. Then again, I'm goth, so what do you expect?

If you're feeling less dramatic about the demise of a deck and/or only some cards are damaged, you can repurpose the undamaged cards for decoupage, collage, mobiles, and other creative endeavors or use them for spellcraft and rituals. Some people prefer to ritually burn or bury a damaged deck, which is certainly one way to put a deck "to rest." But if a fair amount of the deck is still usable for other tasks, the artist in me prefers to make the best of a bad situation.

Tempest's Tarot Thoughts: Musings, Confessions, and Philosophies

I suspect that if you've read this far, you probably have a good idea now of how I approach the Tarot. But you may still have some questions about what I think about the Tarot and my relationship with it beyond playing with numbers, art, and movement. Here are some of my thoughts and opinions.

Am I Predicting the Future? When I read the Tarot, I don't look at it as predicting the future. I use Tarot to look into what has happened, what's going on, and what are the likely outcomes of a situation. I am asking, "What do I need to know about this situation and what can I do about it?" I don't believe that the future is set, that fate is unchanging, and that our lives are destined and predetermined. But I do believe that we have patterns we like to adhere to and there are challenges to our preferred patterns. There's the probability of what can happen, the factors we do know about, and then there are surprises that catch us off guard. I believe we have agency and options in determining our paths. A Tarot reading can help me gain a better understanding of the who, what, when, where, why, and how so that I can make better choices.

How Do I Think the Tarot Works? Do I really think that 78 little cards know and contain the wisdom of the universe? Yes, in a way. The Tarot is a tool for tapping into the universal rhythms we are all a part of—and they can help us gain clarity, just like any tool used properly. They are created by human beings for human beings. I'm also an animist, so I believe that all things contain a certain level of energy and consciousness, including plants, animals, chairs, clothes, and, yes, even Tarot decks. Both animate and inanimate objects are part of the universe, made up of matter set into patterns of atoms. The tools we work with not only have their own mass and matter, set into form by those who made them, but also pick up and intermingle with the energy of those who use them. When something that is made contains a collection of ideas, images, and patterns, not only do those ideas hold power and wisdom symbolically but they also become a tool of communication. This process creates a sense of personality, a vocabulary that you can interact with. The Tarot taps into our collective conscious and unconscious selves, revealing wisdom that was already present within us, and helps to give it a voice we recognize and understand.

I know Tarot reading isn't considered a science, but observation, probability, and examining results are all key ingredients that are part of the process. I like to call my Tarot deck a small "two-by-four"—not because the deck precisely fits those measurements, but more because it tends to be hard and heavy-hitting, like a wooden two-by-four.

What Is Tarot Good For? Tarot is excellent for exploring situations, influences, choices, and options. It can help us explore our own psyches, emotionally, mentally, and spiritually. Tarot is great for inspiration, ritual focus and design, archetype exploration, and spellcraft. You can use Tarot to look at things broadly or in fairly specific detail with the right question and spread.

What Is Tarot *Not* Good For? Tarot is not a replacement for proper therapy, mental health treatment, or prescribed medicine. Questions like "Will I find true love?" can't be solved with the Tarot, but it can be used to investigate what steps you could take to draw a healthy relationship to you.

How Often Do I Have Other People Read for Me? Not often. In fact, very rarely. Maybe I have trust issues, but I'm exceptionally picky about who I let read for me. I've played the role of psychic/priestx/therapist for so many people that it's a bit hard to flip the table. There's also the issue of folks who know me and those who *think* they know me, so there's a certain bias involved. Instead, I tend to consult my own deck as needed—and share my not-Tarot-applicable questions with my actual therapist. I'm not advocating that you do the same, as it can be really important to get an outside perspective or more clarity when you're stuck on something.

Is There Such a Thing as Having Too Many Decks? Between my partner and I, we probably have way too many decks, but we love supporting fellow artists and authors. I especially love the variety of art and the different kinds of approaches. But when it comes to reading, there's just a handful that I read with regularly. If I knew I could keep on top of it, I would love to work with a different deck each week and see where that goes. Every year I go through our decks to see if there are some that should get a new home.

What Was Your First Deck and Do You Still Read with It? Legend: The Arthurian Tarot by Anna-Marie Ferguson was my first deck, and yes, I'm on my second copy. I use it now more for myself than for others, and it rotates with other decks, so it's not my primary deck. But I still have warm fuzzies for it.

What Does It Mean to Be a Tarot Reader? I think Tarot reading and similar divination services provide assistance for living in a stressful world. People want readings to know what's going to happen because they're unsure or confused and want to be reassured that things are going to be all right, to confess or unload what's on their minds, and to work out their issues and desires. Early on, I understood that being a Tarot reader serves the combined role of psychic healer, spiritual guide, and therapist—often without the respect, pay, or education.

What Do You Love Most About Being a Tarot Reader? I love helping people gain insight into themselves and what's happening in their lives. It's wonderful to see people become unstuck and take on a renewed sense of focus after a reading.

What Do You Dislike Most About Being a Tarot Reader? The querents who want a certain outcome and keep asking about it over and over again but will do nothing to actually help themselves achieve that goal. You have to do the work.

The Confessional: What Would I Have Changed Starting Out? As I mentioned previously, I was doing a lot of readings in my early twenties with not a whole lot of life experience and I wanted to make both my clients and the shop happy. I was also in an emotionally and verbally abusive marriage, where the burden of generating income largely fell on me, so there was a huge amount of pressure to make everyone happy to keep the peace. I had clients who became addicted to my readings, and I didn't know what else to do or how to stop it back then. I wish I had been supported and guided to have better boundaries. It would have been a lot healthier for both me and my clients.

Will I Ever Offer Readings Again as a Public Service? While I don't anticipate ever going back to doing readings full-time (my current hare-brained idea of a retirement plan is moving to the desert, creating an artist commune, and raising miniature donkeys—and I don't expect the donkeys will want readings), I still do read professionally on occasion. But I prefer to do one-off events, like the fundraiser for my friend who was running for local office or a welcoming party for freshman at my alma mater. So you can't book me to do regular readings.

———— • ● • ————

Obviously, I can't answer every possible question directly in this book, but I hope your visit to the Hermit's cave has provided you with some mind snacks to chew on for a while. If you come up with a question, you can always use the contact form on my website at www.lauratempestzakroff.com to send in a Tarot question suggestion. If I get enough of them, I may film a video or write a blog post where I try and answer the ones I can tackle. I can't promise that I can answer or respond personally to every question I receive, but they will be collected and saved for possible future explorations.

Conclusion

Divination has likely been part of human existence from the moment we first wondered how the universe worked and what we could do about it. Our ancestors in the caves thousands of years ago likely had systems of divination, and you can find at least one method—if not dozens—in every culture around the world. And each of those methods started with the simplest of approaches and ideas. I think it's important to keep these roots in mind as you continue to build your own practice.

When I look at the Tarot, I see an incredible tool with multiple layers to explore. I also see people who try to make learning and using the Tarot as complex as possible, as if those efforts could enhance its already significant potency. We see this pattern repeated throughout the occult world especially. Far too many people want to believe that for something to be advanced, it must also be complex. Yet time and time again, as a teacher and a practitioner, I have discovered that the opposite is true. Simplicity is the real challenge, as is maintaining a sense of play and imagination.

With the techniques I've shared with you in this book, you can now select any layer and get a good reading. You can use the number system to give you some solid bones for remembering what the cards mean. You can play with the expression of the numbers for another level of meaning: how they interact with each other and how they influence the spread. You can connect the numbers and shapes to feel how they move energetically in a reading—and you can also explore this motion with your own body. You can also find more clues about meaning in the colors, composition, and other symbols—seeing the story play out before your eyes and allowing yourself to interpret the art as it relates to your personal experience. These layers combined empower your journey with the Tarot through the activation of your mind, your body, and your spirit.

I hope you have discovered that this book isn't just about reading the Tarot more effectively. I mean, a huge part of my goal here is to help you connect better with the Tarot. However, the other secret goal of the math is to help you see numbers as a guide to the map of life, a key to unlocking some of life's mysteries and problems—and being able to chart a course to solving them. I am excited that you may look at images and art with new eyes as well, discovering symbolism that expands your wisdom and understanding—not just of the Tarot, but of other aspects of your life and magical practice as well.

Most of all, I hope my approach has helped you see that the rhythm of the Tarot is part of the pattern of life, of the Universe itself—expressed in numbers, symbols, and shapes. You can dress up the practice as much as you'd like, but always remember that you can start by simply tapping into the rhythm of the cards. And just like you, the cards are ever in motion. Enjoy the dance!

Thank you!

~LTZ

Walpurgisnacht 2025

P.S. Go back and look at the chapter numbers and their related topics. I wrote this book without numbering the chapters—I just focused on what I needed to cover for you. But when I went back at the end to number the chapters, I had to laugh, because I think the numbers do work out perfectly!

Acknowledgments

Thanks to Abigail Keyes for helping to double-check and unblock my brain when it came to breaking down the cards.

Thank you to Elysia for your patience while my brain decided to go on hiatus for a couple of months. It's not like there was anything major going on or anything.

Much appreciation to all my students over the years, but especially those who have been so incredibly enthusiastic about my Tarot classes and encouraged me to write this book.

Extra thanks and love to all my Patreon folks who have been joining me online for Zoom almost every week since March 2020. Our work together, especially for our regular "Tarot Time," helped prove proof of concept again and again. Thanks for your questions about the Tarot as well!

Additional gratitude to T. Thorn Coyle and our collective students for the 2024 session of "Invoking the Star," a yearlong study of transformation.

Special thanks to Professor Robert Mathiesen for helping me with the Tarot back in the 1990s—and providing a replacement copy of the Arthurian Tarot. Unbeknownst to him, my own copy had been damaged in a torrential downpour at a festival and then it went out of print. (Llewellyn, you may want to bring it back. I'm just saying.) I'm serious, y'all, when I say ziplock bags, Tarot decks, and outdoor events are a vital and winning combination.

Much appreciation to my early readers for their enthusiasm and insight—and to my mom, who has proofread pretty much every book I have written. Last but absolutely not least, thank you to "my" whole Llewellyn team, from editing and proofing to art, design, and marketing—thank you all for bringing my work to life!

Bibliography

Cavendish, Richard. *The Tarot*. New York: Harper & Row, 1975.

Fiebig, Johannes, and Evelin Burger. *The Ultimate Guide to the Rider Waite Tarot*. Woodbury, MN: Llewellyn, 2016.

Field, Michael, and Martin Golubitsky. *Symmetry in Chaos: A Search for Pattern in Mathematics, Art, and Nature*. New York: Oxford University Press, 1992.

French, Karen L. *The Hidden Geometry of Life: The Science and Spirituality of Nature*. London: Watkins, 2012.

Gray, Eden. *Mastering the Tarot: Basic Lessons in an Ancient, Mystic Art*. New York: Crown, 1975.

Hundley, Jessica. *Tarot*. Los Angeles, CA: Taschen, 2020.

Kaplan, Stuart R. *The Artwork & Times of Pamela Colman Smith*. Stamford, CT: U.S. Games Systems, 2009.

Kaplan, Stuart R. *The Encyclopedia of Tarot, Volume 1*. Stamford, CT: U.S. Games Systems, 1978.

Stewart, Ian. *What Shape Is a Snowflake? Magical Numbers in Nature*. New York: W. H. Freeman, 2001.

Waite, Arthur Edward. *The Pictorial Key to the Tarot*. Stamford, CT: U.S. Games Systems, 2009.

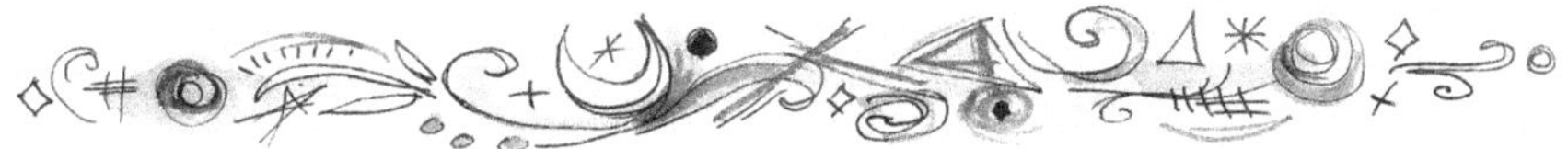

Suggested Resources

I want to share with you some of my favorite decks and other resources to check out to expand your Tarot journey.

A Selection of Recommended Tarot Decks That Are Queer, BIPOC, Unusual, or Otherwise Noteworthy

- *Apophenia Tarot* by Steven Archer
- *Bee Tarot* by Kristoffer Hughes (author) and Nadia Turner (artist)
- *Boadicea's Tarot of Earthly Delights* by Caroline Kenner (author) and Paula Millet (deck creator and artist)
- *The Black Ink Tarot* by Evvie Marin
- *Fifth Spirit Tarot* by Charlie Claire Burgess
- *Fyodor Pavlov Tarot* by Fyodor Pavlov
- *The Gentle Tarot* by Mari in the Sky
- *Lilifer Tarot* by Marion Costentin
- *The Lubanko Tarot* by E. Lubanko
- *The Numinous Tarot* by Cedar McCloud
- *Modern Witch Tarot* by Lisa Sterle
- *The Prisma Visions Tarot* by James R. Eads
- *Rhythm & Soul Tarot* by Stacey Williams-Ng
- *Sasuraibito Tarot* by Stasia Burrington
- *This Might Hurt Tarot* by Isabella Rotman

Further Reading & Exploration

Seventy-Eight Degrees of Wisdom: A Tarot Journey to Self-Awareness by Rachel Pollack (Weiser)

Tarot by Jessica Hundley (Taschen)

The Psychic Art of Tarot: Opening Your Inner Eye for More Insightful Readings by Mat Auryn (Llewellyn)

Radical Tarot: Queer the Cards, Liberate Your Practice, and Create the Future by Charlie Claire Burgess (Hay House)

Tabula idem: A Queer Tarot Comic Anthology edited by Iris Jay and Hye M (360 Digital Books)

Tarot Every Witch Way: Unlock the Power of the Cards for Spellcraft & Magic by Lilith Dorsey (Llewellyn)

Tarot for One: The Art of Reading for Yourself by Courtney Weber (Weiser)

Also check out Benebell Wen's blog and videos for insights into the Tarot world, https://benebellwen.com.

Video Resources

"The Art of Shuffling: An Introduction to Styles & Techniques" by Will Roya: https://playingcarddecks.com/blogs/all-in/the-art-of-shuffling-an-introduction-to-styles-techniques

My YouTube channel: https://www.youtube.com/@LTZWitch

Quick Number Reference

Major Arcana

0	Fool: beginning, wonder
1	Magician: gaining experience
2	High Priestess: dualities, mysteries
3	Empress: creativity, abundance, choices
4	Emperor: foundation, security
5	Hierophant: cycles, spiritual traditions
6	Lovers: motion and movement, what moves our hearts
7	Chariot: pursuit, pulling together opposing forces
8	Strength: balancing physical, emotional, and mental strengths
9	Hermit: rounding toward completion with introspection, consider past/present/future
10	Wheel of Fortune: cycle of fate, starting/ending cycles, completion
11	Justice: balancing effort, understanding complex duality
12	Hanged One: suspension, sacrifice
13	Death: change after sacrifice, clarity
14	Temperance: regaining balance, moderation
15	Devil: trapped by old concepts or toxic habits, revelation of opportunity

16	Tower: cracked foundation, breaking down unhealthy or unstable things
17	Star: possibilities of hope, inspiration
18	Moon: introspection, lunar mysteries
19	Sun: celebration, success
20	Judgement: acknowledgment; a new, wiser cycle
21	World: completion, resolution, clarity

Minor Arcana

1	New start, focus
2	Dualities
3	Choices, possibilities
4	Foundations, balance, stability
5	Cycles, something has to change
6	Journeys, movement
7	Pursuit, opposing forces coming together
8	Capacity for strength and growth
9	Almost there, problem-solving
10	Completion, end of cycle
Page	Messengers, younger/less experienced bringing insight
Knight	Journeys, quests, progression, maturing people
Queen	Nurturing or advising role of suit's energy
King	Guiding or ruling energy of suit's energy

To Write to the Author

If you wish to contact the author or would like more information about this book, please write to the author in care of Llewellyn Worldwide Ltd. and we will forward your request. Both the author and the publisher appreciate hearing from you and learning of your enjoyment of this book and how it has helped you. Llewellyn Worldwide Ltd. cannot guarantee that every letter written to the author can be answered, but all will be forwarded. Please write to:

Laura Tempest Zakroff
℅ Llewellyn Worldwide
2143 Wooddale Drive
Woodbury, MN 55125-2989

Please enclose a self-addressed stamped envelope for reply, or $1.00 to cover costs. If outside the U.S.A., enclose an international postal reply coupon.

Many of Llewellyn's authors have websites with additional information and resources. For more information, please visit our website at https://www.llewellyn.com.